INTRODUCTION TO THE
Theory of Music

INTRODUCTION

TO THE

Theory of Music

HOWARD BOATWRIGHT

DEAN OF THE SCHOOL OF MUSIC

SYRACUSE UNIVERSITY

W · W · NORTON & COMPANY · INC · New York

Library of Congress Catalog Card No. 56-11456

ISBN 0 393 02057 6

PRINTED IN THE UNITED STATES OF AMERICA

3 4 5 6 7 8 9

To Helen

Contents

PART TWO
Scales and Melody
PROJECTS IN MELODY WRITING

Preface

This book is a general introduction to the technical aspects of music. Beginning with the assumption that the student has had no previous training, it prepares him for the more advanced subjects of theory, such as harmony, counterpoint, and orchestration. It deals with basic terminologies and problems of notation (the "rudiments of music"), it supplies material for developing the fundamental skills of performance ("ear-training," "sight-singing," etc.), and through the study of scales and melody it builds a foundation for harmony and counterpoint. The appendixes introduce some of the principles of abstract acoustical theory, discuss the instruments of the orchestra from the point of view of the score-reader, and provide for reference a glossary of foreign terms and lists of miscellaneous signs and abbreviations. Although it has been conceived mainly as a text for classroom use, this book may also be used profitably by the general reader who wishes to learn about the elements of music; and its glossary and index may be used as convenient references on rudimentary technical matters.

Like many other texts, this book was originally developed in the classroom. It is not, however, simply a written-out course; for the book has broader and more general lines than the class material from which it grew. It covers the whole area of introductory theory more thoroughly than the original outlines, and it should therefore be adaptable to the varying demands of other teachers and students.

The body of the text contains enough material for a full year's course. Yet the author was not unaware that many teachers, especially in liberal arts programs, cannot devote a whole year to introductory matters, since they cannot count on having a second full year for harmony, which is nearly always the subject closest to the core of the student's interest in music theory. Nevertheless, most teachers need introductory material, as college students are seldom ready at the beginning to study harmony; and this text will serve them well if its procedures are shortened whenever necessary. On the other hand, in a program for music majors a full year could be devoted to the performance problems of Part I alone, leaving the material on scales and melody to the first months of a second year course. In organizing this book, the author tried to take into account the different kinds of demands likely to be made upon it; and the book is so arranged that it may be shortened by omitting some of the written work, or expanded by increasing the number of exercises, according to the needs of the particular course. The teacher should not feel that any required sequence is imposed upon him; he is free to use the book as a whole or only in part, and in any sequence his own ingenuity may suggest.

Every book has its idiosyncrasies; and one which may be observed in this text is the juxtaposition of purely practical matters (how to recognize an interval, how to perform a rhythm) with historical or abstract theoretical discussions (early chant, troubadours, equal temperament, etc.). This juxtaposition results to some extent from concurrent use of the same material for two quite different groups: a first year class in the Yale School of Music (a professional school) and an introductory theory class in Yale College (a liberal arts college). It seemed to the author that each of these groups might benefit from the approach more usual for the other. Ordinarily the professional student is interested in developing his practical skills, and pays little attention to the historical background or the theoretical horizons of his subject. The liberal arts student, on the other hand, is likely to read, think, and talk about all aspects of a subject, but fall short in actual practice. An approach combining practical, theoretical, and historical information, emphasized in that order, will both broaden the background of the professional student and anchor the roving inquisitiveness of the undergraduate to a practical base.

Here again, the teacher is free to emphasize or reduce the importance of any element. He may, for instance, use the brief historical sections as starting points for more thorough discussions, with assigned reading in appropriate sources. Or, he may expand the abstract theoretical sections into more detailed investigations, which could, in some cases, lead to discussions of the trends of contemporary music. Or, should he so desire, he may give all of these matters a minimum of attention, and concentrate on the development of practical musicianship.

A book ought to have a better reason for existence than the mere repetition of material which has already been presented many times before. But the more familiar the subject, the less likely that anything new can be added, although old material can sometimes be advantageously rearranged. What can be new in the elementary facts of music? and what material can be advantageously rearranged now?

In some aspects of theory—notation, for example—there are no particularly new points of view, and rearrangement may not necessarily produce better results than have been previously obtained. But the manner in which present day composers handle tonal and rhythmical material does indicate the need at this time for new theoretical formulations and for new treatments of some subjects which have long been approached in standardized ways. These new formulations and treatments ought to result naturally from the sifting down of advanced composition practices to the lower level of elementary theory—a process which so far has occurred in only negligible proportions.

Consider, for instance, the subject of scales. Elementary theory usually presents only the system of major and minor keys, and even that without regard to its particular origin, or its limitations. But for more than half a century now, leading composers have written a kind of music which by no means stays within the bounds of the major and minor scale system. Furthermore, the recent growth of interest in the music of composers earlier than Bach, brought about to a large extent by recordings, has made regular listening fare of music based on tonal systems which preceded major and minor. For these reasons, it would seem plainly necessary nowadays to give scales a much broader treatment than they have usually received in elementary books. Adequate treatment of scales would lay the foundation for an approach to contemporary theory and develop even in students not expecting to proceed further a flexible and unprejudiced perceptivity, enabling them to respond more readily to musical styles which do not conform exactly to the major and minor system.

Other aspects of the thinking of contemporary composers also suggest changes in procedure at lower levels. The freer attitude of our time with regard to scales is accompanied by an approach to harmony which is quite different from the previous fixed conception of chord-building in thirds. The simplest definition of a chord which is in keeping with contemporary usage is that it is three or more tones in vertical order—any tones in any order, selected by the composer according to his desire for greater or lesser dissonance and his over-all conception of harmonic organization. Although we would not deal with the problems of harmony in an elementary book, old or new in approach, our attitude about harmony will determine how we treat the study of intervals, which is one of the regular parts of elementary theory.

In the conventional approach, chords and scales are considered as pre-existing, inviolate units. Intervals, therefore can be derived from them and learned after the more complex units have been presented. But if we wish to prepare the student for melodies which do more than crawl safely up and down the well-known ladders, or for chords which freely use the wide variety of possible tone combinations, we must realize that intervals are the only constant tonal units, and we must, therefore, begin at the earliest stages to develop an independent sense for them. Intervals must have a more thorough treatment than they can possibly receive when they are inserted between discussions of scales and chords at relatively late stages of theory training. Furthermore, to approach intervals before scales or chords has a certain innate logic, as scales and chords are and always have been derivations from intervals.

Just as the interval is the common tonal unit for all forms of scales and chords, so is the "beat," or metric unit, the common element for all forms of measures and higher rhythmical structures. Contemporary composers exercise the utmost freedom with regard to meter—no longer caring to fit whole movements into any one scheme—and in matters of higher rhythmical thinking (phrases, etc.) they are

given to no regular system, such as counting bars in groups of
four, eight, or sixteen. (Again, the same points of view are apparent
in early music.) If we apply these attitudes to an elementary study
of rhythm, we will see that the first thing the student must learn
is not the $\frac{3}{4}$ or $\frac{4}{4}$ measure, which he then fills in with notes, but a
feeling for the beat itself and the many kinds of rhythmic patterns
which may fill the beat. He can, after achieving this, easily deal with
the arrangements of the beats into groups of three, four, five, or any
other metrical schemes. As for the phraseology of the measures
themselves, nothing has to be done, as this is a very unclear area in
music theory, and will most likely remain so. But at least the implication that there is a normal and fixed length for higher rhythmical
units can be avoided by omitting the usual discussions of phrase organization by four or its multiples.

The article on Music Theory in the *Harvard Dictionary of Music*
lists the commonly taught subjects and points out that "at least one
important study is missing, that of melody." This condition is
simply a reflection of the attitudes of composers who in styles of
the fairly recent past failed to treat melody as an independent entity because of their greater interest in the expressive and constructive force of harmony. Melody, in fact, often became a mere
derivation from chords, the more ancient and subtle element being
overpowered by the younger and more dynamic one.

In our own time, however, harmony has become a more flexible
element, perhaps less able to serve as a frame for the construction
of melodies, but better able than ever to underscore independent
melodic flights. And a melody (like a chord) may be simply but
inclusively defined as: a chain of intervals in horizontal succession—
any intervals in any order, according to the composer's desire for
height or depth in the melodic curve and his over-all conception of
tonal organization.

If melody is now free from the direct influence of harmony, as it
was in the distant past, then the study of melody need no longer
be delayed until after the study of harmony, when in any case, it is
likely to be overshadowed. If a melodic line is a chain of intervals,
why not study melody in connection with learning intervals? If
melodic lines have rhythmic shape, why not at this stage bring up

questions of musical form, since these questions can then be discussed in the simplest and clearest way, without the distraction of harmony? If a knowledge of scales is a prerequisite for advanced study, why not acquire this knowledge by using scales for melody-writing? All of these things can be done if it is once agreed that melody need not wait upon harmony.

The question is, what sort of melodic study should be attempted —an abstract examination of the nature of melody without regard to style, or one based entirely on stylistic imitation? This question and a proposed solution are discussed at some length in Chapter 10. The treatment of pure nonchordal melody in a beginning text, of course, can be neither profound nor exhaustive. But the fact that any kind of treatment is offered has some significance; it indicates a radical shift of emphasis, derived from the application of a contemporary point of view to elementary study.

If we accept the arguments presented above, we will agree that the study of elementary theory can and should be affected by changes in the practice of composition. Also, if the approach to basic matters is adjusted to conform to the contemporary outlook, it also comes into better focus with the music of earlier times, which by coincidence (if nothing more than this) is enjoying a new popularity. But would a reshuffling of the order of presentation, and various shifts in emphasis, cause elementary theory to lose its connection with the music of common practice—the music of the classical and romantic periods?

It would not; simply because the vital element in the theoretical background for the music of the familiar period is the subject of harmony, and this subject will still come after the early stages of training. The modification of harmony's influence upon early training, and an intensification of the study of intervals and scales, as well as rhythm, cannot but have a beneficial effect upon later study, as they impose upon the pre-harmony student a higher than usual level of achievement in basic matters before he faces the complexities of harmony. And it is also true that rudimentary definitions given entirely within the narrow frame of traditional practice set up artificial barriers which must later be removed; while definitions given within the wider scope of both ancient and contemporary

practice keep the way open from the start for steady and uninter-
rupted progress.

This elementary text cannot pretend to make a grand entrance
into the vast and almost completely empty arena of contemporary
theory. But the author hopes that by establishing a broader point
of view at the start, the book will, within its limits, contribute something toward that reconciliation of theory and practice which is
now so long overdue.

Howard Boatwright

Yale University
New Haven, Connecticut

Acknowledgements

The author wishes to extend grateful acknowledgement to his friends and colleagues at Yale University and in the Yale School of Music who have helped in various ways with this book. Dr. George Lam, literary historian and musician as well, gave invaluable assistance with several early mimeographed versions of the manuscript. Dean Luther Noss and Professors Richard Donovan and Quincy Porter read the manuscript at a later stage and made a number of helpful suggestions. Special assistance with Appendix II was provided by Professor Keith Wilson, and with Appendix IV by Professor Luigi Silva. Professor James F. M. Stephens of the Department of French kindly supplied the unrhymed translations of the medieval French song texts in Chapter XIII. For other helpful favors, the author also wishes to thank Professors William G. Waite and Norman H. Pearson.

The drawings of the stringed instruments, woodwinds, brass instruments, timpani, and drums are by Paul M. Boatwright.

Maxwell Weaner autographed all the musical examples except the score pages in Appendix III.

Mr. Ezra Pound gave his kind permission for the use of two translated poems from *The Spirit of Romance* (London, J. W. Dent, 1932), on pages 163–164.

Finally, the author wishes to express his thanks to the staff of W. W. Norton—especially Mr. Robert Farlow and Mrs. Richard Fried—for many suggestions which led to improvements, and for their uncompromising perfectionism in the production of the book.

H.B.

PART ONE

Intervals and Rhythms
PROBLEMS OF PERFORMANCE, PERCEPTION, AND NOTATION

CHAPTER

⚚1⚚

Intervals

An isolated tone, sounded all by itself, is capable of very little musical effect; only some unusual feature of loudness, softness, harshness, or smoothness could cause it to have any meaning for us. But if we add to this isolated tone another one, either sounding at the same time or following it in succession, a more definite although still elementary effect will be produced, and we will have formed one of the basic two-note combinations from which all larger tonal groupings must be derived.

In our music there are twelve of these basic two-note combinations, and our first problem will be to learn to sing and to recognize them, and to become aware of their various effects. We shall make a direct approach to this problem by means of exercises, minimizing most of the details of notation until the voice and ear have been awakened to their tasks.

The basic two-note combinations which we must learn to sing and recognize are called *intervals*. This term is derived from the well-known analogy between the high and low of physical space and the high and low of musical pitch; it refers to the distances between the tones in musical "space," or what we might more precisely call "pitch-space."

We recognize intervals in two forms. When the tones are sounded in succession they are a unit of melody, and we say that the interval is in *melodic* form. When the tones are sounded together they are a unit of harmony, and we say that the interval is in *harmonic* form.

In conjunction with the demonstration and definition of the twelve basic intervals we shall also have occasion to examine the structure of the piano keyboard, which, since the piano is the commonest musical tool of all uses, will provide us with visual and tonal aids, both in demonstration and in practice.

STEPS

The smallest interval is called a *half-step*, or *half-tone* (symbol: H). It may be found, counting both white and black keys, between any two adjacent notes of the piano.

EXPERIMENT 1.

a. Select a tone on the keyboard which is within the range of your voice. For men, this would be a little to the left of the center of the keyboard; for women, a little to the right of the center.

b. Play this tone and the next adjacent tone to the right. Sing what you have played. This is the ascending half-step. Then play and sing the original tone and the next adjacent tone to the left. This produces the descending half-step.

c. Select another tone within your voice range. After striking this tone, try to *think* the half-step above or below, and sing the pitch you have in mind. Check yourself by playing the correct note.

The next smallest interval is the *whole-step*, or *whole-tone* * (symbol: W), which may be found on the piano by omitting one key (again counting both black and white ones) between those that are played.

EXPERIMENT 2.

Follow the same procedures as in Experiment 1 in learning to play and sing whole-steps.

TONAL ORDERS ON THE KEYBOARD

Even a casual glance at the piano keyboard will reveal that the arrangement of keys conforms to a certain symmetrical pattern. Actually this pattern expresses three different tonal orders.

---

* Another terminology, less useful than the ones given here because of possible ambiguity, refers to a whole-step as a *tone*, and a half-step as a *semitone*.

If we brush our hands across the black keys, we sound the tones of the *pentatonic* order. If we do likewise across the white keys, we sound the *diatonic* order. If we could brush our hands across the black and white keys together, we would produce the *chromatic* order.

The number of tones contained in each of the three orders provides us with a rudimentary idea as to their relative complexities. The pentatonic order is the simplest since it contains the smallest number of tones. The chromatic order is the most complicated for the opposite reason: it contains the maximum number of tones. The most important order for us is the moderately complicated diatonic, because the majority of our music falls into that category.

THE OCTAVE

Since our music is mainly diatonic, most of the terms used to define tonal distances (intervals) are derived from counting within that order; the intervals received names based on the number of diatonic tones contained within them. For example, the interval called an *octave* (Latin: *octo*, eight) spans eight of the diatonic white keys of the piano.

EXPERIMENT 3.

a. Play a white key which sounds a pitch within the lower part of your voice range. After you find an appropriate note, count upward to the eighth white key and play this tone. Then try to sing the octave *leap* you have played. (All melodic intervals other than the two steps are referred to as "leaps.")

b. Selecting a white key high in your voice range, play and sing a descending octave leap.

It will be observed at once that the two tones of an octave sound like mirror images of each other. The repetitive pattern of the keyboard conforms in construction to this natural fact. The eighth tone of a diatonic pattern occupies a position among the keys exactly parallel to that of the first tone.

EXPERIMENT 4.

a. Play a white key located between two black keys. Count to the eighth white key above. This tone will also lie between two black keys.

b. Play other octaves, and observe the symmetry of the keyboard patterns.

DEFINITIONS OF PENTATONIC, DIATONIC, AND CHROMATIC

With the perspective gained on the keyboard from the above experiments, and with the help of the one which follows, we can now offer explanations for the terms which define the three tonal orders.

EXPERIMENT 5.

a. How many pentatonic tones are there within an octave? (Count only the black keys.)

b. How many chromatic tones are there within an octave? (Count both white and black keys.)

The name "pentatonic" (Greek: *pénte*, five) obviously derives from the number of tones within an octave. The reasons for the names of the other two orders, however, are not so direct. "Diatonic" is from the Latin *diatonicus*. The Greek prefix *dia* in this word means "through," or "across," implying, therefore, that this order goes through or across all the tones. "Chromatic" is from the Latin *chromaticus*, which, again, has a Greek connection. The Greek *chroma* means "color." The earliest chromatic elements in music were produced by altering, adding to, or "coloring" the diatonic tones. The chromatic order retains the name which originated at a time when it was regarded only as a derivation from, or coloration of, the diatonic order.

THE GAMUT

Since the range of the piano keyboard far exceeds that of human voices, we may define the tonal area for our present experiments within much narrower limits. A two-octave range, or *gamut*, will suffice. For male voices we may begin this gamut (starting from the bottom) at the second octave duplication of the lowest note on the keyboard. For female voices we may begin at the third octave duplication.

Our gamut will extend upward from this point through all the white keys of two octaves. The whole pattern should look like this:

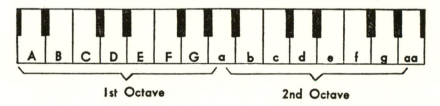

The first seven letters of the alphabet are used to name the seven different diatonic tones. Capitals are used for the lower octave, and small letters for the upper. The last tone is a double small letter.

EXPERIMENT 6.

a. Locate the gamut on the piano and play the tones. Between what notes do half-steps occur? How many half-steps can you find within any one octave?

b. Sing as much of the gamut as you can, checking yourself at the piano. Observe how it relates to your voice range. Its lowest notes will be too low for high voices (tenors and sopranos) and its highest notes too high for low voices (basses and altos).

With the tones of a two-octave gamut at our disposal we can now find and demonstrate the remaining intervals—those which lie between the sizes of the largest step and the octave, and also some of those which exceed the octave.

OTHER INTERVALS

Just as the octave derives its name from diatonic counting, so do the other intervals. If we play three diatonic steps in succession, the outer tones span the interval of a *third*.

EXPERIMENT 7.

Mark all whole- and half-steps (e.g., A - B - C), and play and sing
                                             ‿‿ ‿‿
                                             W H
the following patterns:

1. A-B-C, A-C-A

2. B-C-D, B-D-B

3. C-D-E, C-E-C

4. D-E-F, D-F-D

5. E-F-G, E-G-E

6. F-G-a, F-a-F

7. G-a-b, G-b-G

It will be observed that there are two different sizes of thirds; one spans two whole-steps and the other spans only one whole- and one half-step. The two sizes are distinguished from each other by the use of the qualifying terms *major* for the large one (symbol: M3) and *minor* for the small one (symbol: m3). Mark the thirds in the diagram above with symbols (e.g., E-G-E or G-b-G).
                                                ‿‿‿ ‿‿‿
                                                m3   M3

By the same terminology the whole- and half-steps may also be called *major* and *minor seconds* (symbols: M2, m2). This designation applies mainly when they occur in harmonic form.

We may carry out the same experiment with the next largest interval.

EXPERIMENT 8.

Construct *fourths,* playing and singing the following patterns.
Mark the steps first.

1. A-B-C-D,   A-D-A

2. B-C-D-E,   B-E-B

3. C-D-E-F,   C-F-C

4. D-E-F-G,   D-G-D

5. E-F-G-a,   E-a-E

6. F-G-a-b,   F-b-F

7. G-a-b-c,   G-c-G

In this case we find only one interval which differs in size from
the others. It differs so greatly in sound as to belong to an entirely
separate class of intervals from the other fourths, which are smooth
and pleasant in their effect. We must therefore use a different set of
qualifying terms from those applied to the thirds. We call the
normal fourths *perfect* (symbol: 4), and the off-color fourth *augmented,* since it is a half-step larger than the others.

Another special name for the augmented fourth is *tritone;* it
spans three whole-tones. An advantage of this term over the other
one is that it does not suggest derivation from the normal fourth,
but treats this interval as the independent entity that it really is. It
is from the name "tritone" that we take the symbol for an augmented fourth: T.

Mark the leaps in the diagram with appropriate symbols.

Fifths may be examined by the following experiment:

EXPERIMENT 9.

After marking the steps, play and sing these patterns:

1. A-B-C-D-E,   A-E-A

2. B-C-D-E-F,   B-F-B

3. C-D-E-F-G, C-G-C

4. D-E-F-G-a, D-a-D

5. E-F-G-a-b, E-b-E

6. F-G-a-b-c, F-c-F

7. G-a-b-c-d, G-d-G

With the fifths we again find only one out-of-place interval. This time the misfit is smaller than all the others. Following the same procedure as with the fourth, we call the normal sizes *perfect* (symbol: 5), and the small size *diminished*.

It may already have been observed that in sound the diminished fifth is identical with the augmented fourth. Although it occurs in a different part of the octave, it is actually the same size as the augmented fourth.

Augmented fourth: 3 whole-steps = 6 half-steps
Diminished fifth: 2 whole-steps, 2 half-steps = 6 half-steps

The name "tritone" may be applied also to the diminished fifth, providing a common name and symbol for these intervals which are so similar in sound.

Mark the leaps in the diagram above with appropriate symbols.

We continue in the same manner with the next interval, the *sixth:*

EXPERIMENT 10.

Mark the steps, and play and sing these patterns:

1. A-B-C-D-E-F, A-F-A

2. B-C-D-E-F-G, B-G-B

3. C-D-E-F-G-a, C-a-C

4. D-E-F-G-a-b, D-b-D

5. E-F-G-a-b-c, E-c-E

6. F-G-a-b-c-d, F-d-F

7. G-a-b-c-d-e, G-e-G

The sixths, like the thirds, are definitely of two sizes; thus the major-minor terminology is applied. The *major sixth* (M6) contains four whole-steps and one half-step. The *minor sixth* (m6) contains three whole-steps and two half-steps. Mark the leaps in the diagram.

The *sevenths* are also of two sizes, as the following experiment will show:

EXPERIMENT 11.

Play and sing the patterns below, marking the steps in advance:

1. A-B-C-D-E-F-G,   A-G-A
2. B-C-D-E-F-G-a,   B-a-B
3. C-D-E-F-G-a-b,   C-b-C
4. D-E-F-G-a-b-c,   D-c-D
5. E-F-G-a-b-c-d,   E-d-E
6. F-G-a-b-c-d-e,   F-e-F
7. G-a-b-c-d-e-f,   G-f-G

The *minor seventh* (m7) contains four whole- and two half-steps, while the *major seventh* (M7) contains five whole-steps and one half-step. Mark the sevenths in the diagram above.

Intervals larger than an octave (sometimes called *compound intervals*) are named by the same method, although the terminology gets so complicated after the thirteenth that it is common to refer to intervals larger than this (and sometimes even the ninth through the thirteenth) by the names of their smaller equivalents within an octave.

EXPERIMENT 12.

a. What are the names of the following intervals? Count them upward from A:

1. An octave + a fifth.
2. "   "   + a third.
3. "   "   + a second.

Count from B:

1. An octave + a second.
2. "   "   + a sixth.
3. "   "   + a fourth.

CLASSIFICATIONS OF INTERVALS

If we regard the two forms of the tritone as a single interval, there are twelve basic intervals * from the octave to the minor second. Arranged in order of size they are:

8 M7 m7 M6 m6 5 T 4 M3 m3 M2 m2.

Graded as to the "smoothness" with which they fall on the ear, the intervals assume the following order, which has traditionally been divided into three classes:

Smooth --------------------increasingly harsher -------------------
   8 5 4   M6 M3 m3 m6   m7 M2 M7 m2 T

Perfect   Imperfect   Dissonances
Consonances †   Consonances

While the gradation of the intervals from smooth to harsh is based on considerations deriving from physics, and is more or less absolute, the application of adjectives like "consonant" and "dissonant" is somewhat subject to change in various musical periods. For example, at an early point in Western musical culture (before about 1300) a third was regarded as a harsh sound, and only perfect consonances were considered to be fully pleasing. But in our own time, through the process of conditioning, some of the intervals still classified as dissonances have lost much of their impact, and no longer impress us as "harsh" except in relation to the simpler intervals.

Since our attention is incapable of focusing on different things with an equal degree of interest, we tend to hear one note of an in-

---

* If two people sing the same tone, a *unison* or *prime* is formed. This is, strictly speaking, not an interval, as that term clearly derives from the distance between different tones. Nevertheless, the unison is sometimes included in interval charts.

† The terms *concord* and *discord* are synonymous with *consonance* and *dissonance*.

terval as more prominent than the other. We call the most prominent note the *root*.

In the case of the highly consonant fifth and fourth the roots are
easily identifiable. The lower note of a fifth is the more prominent,
and the upper note of a fourth stands out.

The octave and the tritone remain outside any classification of
interval roots. There is no need to decide the root of an octave since
the tones are the same. The dissonance and the fact that out of an
actual musical context we cannot tell if it is an augmented fourth or
diminished fifth prevent us from deciding the root of a tritone.

The roots of the other intervals become less clear approximately
as they become more dissonant. They are determined mainly on the
basis of the observed behavior of the intervals in context.

Those intervals which have roots fall together in pairs, since each
interval with its root above is an *inversion* of an interval with its
root below. For instance, if we move the lower tone of a fifth to a
position in the next higher octave, the interval of a fourth is formed:

Fifth   Fourth

Intervals with roots below are somewhat more stable in sound
than those with roots above. This feeling may be some sort of carry-
over from our experiences with real objects in space. The following
diagram shows the balance of root-weight in the fifth and fourth. If
these were real objects we would say that the one with its weight
nearer the bottom was the more stable:

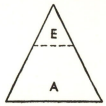 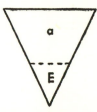

Since complexity results both from harshness and from the feeling
of instability, the following chart (when read according to the arrows) ranges from simple to complex:

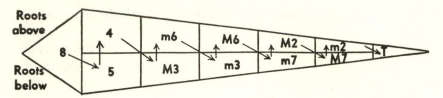

Intervals with odd numbers—3, 5, 7—have roots below. Intervals with even numbers—2, 4, 6—have roots above.

INTERVAL PRACTICE

As a guide for practice, construct a table showing between which tones of the gamut each interval may be found. In starting to make your table, refer to the lists of intervals given in earlier experiments: Experiments 7 (thirds), 8 (fourths), 9 (fifths), 10 (sixths), and 11 (sevenths). The intervals in these experiments were all based on the lower seven tones of the gamut. Don't forget to include the intervals from the upper octave. For seconds (steps) consult the keyboard diagram of the gamut (page 7).

EXPERIMENT 13.

List the tones between which are found:

m2	M2	m3	M3	4	T	5	m6	M6	m7	M7

Learn this table so well that you immediately associate the names of the tones with the correct intervals. For example, one must know without hesitation that E-c is a minor sixth, C-a is a major sixth, F-b is a tritone, and so forth. Such knowledge, combined with a similarly accurate feeling for the *sounds* * of the intervals, is our present goal.

We can make use of this table as an aid in learning the sounds of the intervals through the following experiment:

EXPERIMENT 14.

a. Referring to the table, play and sing intervals, emphasizing those you consider most difficult.

b. Test yourself as in Experiment 1, *c:* play one tone of a given interval, try to imagine the second tone, sing it, and check yourself by playing the second tone.

The importance of the exercises which involve singing cannot be overemphasized: the feeling for intervals is very closely connected with the muscular sensations involved in producing them.

One of the best ways to practice intervals is to take them down by dictation. Such exercises provide a valuable means of checking one's progress, and they have an advantage over some other forms of practice in that they work equally well for small or large groups.

Here is a procedure for dictation:

EXPERIMENT 15.

The person who will dictate prepares lists of intervals selected from the chart of Experiment 13. He chooses his lists according to the needs of the group. The listeners take down the intervals using the symbols (an exceptional person may also be able to take down the names of the notes).

Some suggested schemes, with examples, are:

1. *All perfect consonances*
   5 (A-E), 4 (G-c), 5 (D-a), 4 (B-E), 5 (E-b), 4 (D-G)

2. *Major and minor thirds*
   M (F-a), m (B-D), M (c-e), m (d-f), m (a-c), m (E-G), M (G-b), m (b-d).

---

* A great help in learning intervals is to find examples among known melodies which can be instantly recalled. No list is given here because every person should have his own melody repertoire as a basis.

3. *Major and minor sixths*
   M (C-a), M (G-e), M (D-b), m (E-c), m (A-F), M (c-aa),
   m (B-G), M (F-d).

4. *All imperfect consonances*
   m3 (D-F), M3 (F-a), M6 (C-a), m6 (E-c), M3 (F-a),
   m3 (B-D), m6 (A-F), M6 (D-b).

5. *All consonances, perfect and imperfect*
   5 (C-G), M3 (F-a), M6 (G-e), m3 (A-C), 4 (b-e),
   m6 (E-c), 5 (G-d), 4 (c-f).

6. *Major and minor sevenths*
   M (C-b), m (D-c), m (A-G), M (F-e), M (C-b), m (G-f),
   m (B-a), m (E-d).

7. *Major and minor seconds* (also play as ninths—upper tone an
   octave higher)
   M (A-B), M (c-d), m (B-C), m (E-F), M (F-G), M (G-a),
   m (b-c), M (d-e).

8. *All dissonances* (including the tritone)
   m7 (D-c), T (B-F), m2 (B-C), M7 (F-e), M2 (C-D),
   T (b-f), m7 (E-d), M7 (C-b).

9. *Combinations of all types*
   5 (E-b), m7 (A-G), M3 (F-a), 4 (G-c), T (b-f), m6 (E-c),
   4 (C-F), m3 (b-d).

Dictate the intervals both melodically and harmonically at first.
Here is a form:

a. Play melodically.

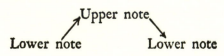

(or the reverse)

Sound the melodic form twice, with a slight pause between
playings.

b. Play harmonically.
Strike the tones together, and let the hands remain on the keys
for a short time to sustain the sound. One playing of the harmonic
form should suffice.

Later on the intervals may be sounded only harmonically. But
in whatever manner they are played, the listener should hum the

melodic form (as in *a*) quietly to himself before making his decision.

It is especially important to learn not to invert the intervals when singing them. Be sure the right tone is on the bottom.

Further complications may be introduced into these exercises by dictating intervals from positions on the keyboard outside the gamut, and by separating the tones by an octave or more. However, such problems should be reserved until some degree of accuracy is achieved within the more normal ranges. When the more difficult exercises are attempted the listener should continue to hum the intervals as before, using the most comfortable equivalents within his own voice range. This helps to establish contact with these more or less disembodied sounds.

CHAPTER

2

Rhythmic Patterns

Our feeling for intervals is dependent upon the pitch-measuring powers of certain tiny organs inside the ear. But on what does our feeling for patterns in time depend?

We have no one sense-organ capable of measuring time. Rather, we relate temporal events to various kinds of bodily experience, such as the beating of the heart, breathing, walking, running, and so forth. All these functions of the body are characterized by some more or less regular ebb and flow.

Certain kinds of music contain enough internal pulsation to awaken an immediate similar response within us as we listen to it. We feel the urge to move some part of the body to which the speed of the pulsations would be natural. For instance, if they are fast, we may want to tap our feet; or if they are slow, we may find ourselves responding with a swaying motion of the body.

Our capacity to respond kinaesthetically to music is the means by which we achieve, when necessary for purposes of notation and performance, a regulation of uneven time lengths. With a certain amount of training we are able to maintain a feeling of regular pulsations within ourselves even when the music invokes no such feelings, and against these steady pulsations we are able accurately to measure any irregular time lengths which may occur.

THE METRICAL ELEMENT: BEAT, TEMPO

The regular recurrent pulsations which we feel in music, or which we impose upon it when necessary, are called *beats*. Because they are regular, the beats serve as the *metrical* element of the temporal structure (Greek: *metron*, measure).

The term *tempo* (Italian: time) refers to the speed of the beats.

We seem to derive our conception of tempo in music from our pulse. Slow tempos are less, and fast tempos are more than 72–80 beats per minute, which is approximately the normal speed of the heartbeat.*

There are thresholds beyond which we find it difficult or impossible to produce or respond to beats. These are tempos which are less than half, or more than twice the speed of the pulse (i.e., below 36 or above 144). Our usual reaction to such tempos is to multiply or divide the beats by two, in order to bring them nearer to our easiest level of response. For example, omitting every other beat would bring a tempo of 220 down to a more intelligible 110. Or supplying an extra beat between those of a tempo of 34 would bring it up to a much more reasonable 68.

EXPERIMENT 16.

a. Locate your pulse over your heart, or on your throat, with your left hand. Wave your right hand in this tempo, which will be about 72–80.

b. Try beating (waving your hand) at twice the speed of your pulse. At three times the speed of your pulse. Try also to beat at one half, and at one third the speed of your pulse.

THE RHYTHMICAL ELEMENT: MULTIPLICATION, DIVISION

The above experiment introduces new temporal events which are free of the beats, yet are regulated by them. These events are the *rhythmical* element of the musical structure (Greek: *rhythmos*, measured motion).

The rhythmical element may stand in two relationships to the metrical element. The rhythmical events may be:

1. Slower than the beats. We call these *multiplications.*
2. Faster than the beats. We call these *divisions.*

* There are ticking devices called *metronomes* which may be adjusted to give any speed between about 30 and 220. The older type using a spring motor (in-

Multiplications are not difficult to perform unless they are complicated by problems of notation. But divisions in their many varieties are much more problematical. Like the singing and recognition of intervals, facility in performing all kinds of divisions has always been regarded as one of the essentials of musicianship.

We shall therefore practice exercises which touch upon most of the common patterns resulting from division, hoping to develop a basic vocabulary which will stand in somewhat the same relationship to larger temporal structures as the isolated interval vocabulary does to larger units in tone.

RHYTHMIC PRACTICE

For our exercises we shall adopt a rudimentary notation. A vertical line will be a sound, and a horizontal line a silence. Here is a rhythmic pattern formed by a division of a beat into three parts, using both sound and silence:

| - |
Sound Silence Sound

We will practice the patterns by repeating them in chains over the duration of a number of beats, which may be shown by vertical arrows. The patterns may be performed by tapping the sounds with a pencil and clapping the beats with the other hand. It is useful to interchange the functions of the hands from time to time. Here is a complete example:

The divisions of beats which occur most often are those into two, three, four, and six parts. Divisions into five and seven parts are more or less exceptional. Larger divisions such as eight and nine tend to break down into smaller ones (4 + 4, and 3 + 3 + 3), and numbers still larger than this require either a beat that is too slow or an execution that is too fast for practicality. Our problems, then, will be limited to the four commonest divisions.

vented by Maelzel in 1816) is being replaced nowadays by new types which use electricity.

EXPERIMENT 17.

a. Practice the following patterns in the manner suggested:

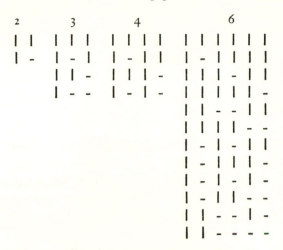

b. Practice these patterns, which are more difficult than the first group. In some of them the first sound is missing, and they are generally more broken up by silences than the others. Chains of patterns in which the first sound is missing produce the kind of rhythm known as *syncopation* (Greek: *synkopē*, a cutting up).

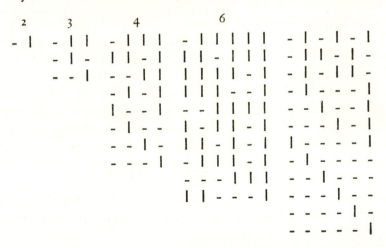

c. Using the patterns given above, practice dictation exercises in order to be sure that the ability to discriminate in listening keeps pace with the ability to perform.

CHAPTER

3

Staff Notation

Although a system of notation by letters alone such as we employed in Chapter 1 is specific enough, it does not convey an immediate visual impression of the relative height and depth of the tones in musical space. The complete modern system brings out the spatial element by placing the tones against a graphlike background of horizontal lines.

The credit for inventing modern notation is sometimes given to Guido d'Arezzo (995–1050), a Benedictine monk who was one of the greatest theorists of the Middle Ages. Actually Guido simply brought into definite form principles which were already in existence before his time.

Guido used three or four horizontal lines. Each line and each space between the lines represented a tone of the gamut. Since the whole gamut was not shown but only a given segment of five to seven tones, a letter was placed in the margin next to one of the lines to indicate the position of either F or c. Color was also employed, with the F line in red, and the c line in yellow or green. From the locations of these two tones the positions of the others could easily be deduced.

The notation we use today has not actually varied in principle from the tenth-century practices described by Guido.

THE STAFF, LEDGER LINES

In modern notation we use a group of five lines, called the *staff* (sometimes *stave*). The staff lines and the spaces between them are counted upward.

The lines and spaces of the staff can represent only nine tones of the gamut. But tones may be placed above or below the staff by

22

adding short lines for each note as needed. The added lines are called *ledger lines.*

CLEFS, BRACES

The F and c which were indicated by Guido have been greatly modified into signs which we call *clefs* (Latin: *clavis*, key):

F is shown as 𝄢

c is shown as 𝄡

Another clef indicating g of the gamut has been added:

g is shown as 𝄞

All three of these clefs were originally movable to various lines of the staff. But in modern practice we use the g clef only on the second line, the F clef on the fourth line, and the c clef on either the third or fourth lines. The F clef and the c clef in its two positions are named according to the three lower vocal ranges to which they are appropriate—*bass, tenor,* and *alto.* The name *treble,* used for the clef appropriate to the soprano voice, is an old English derivation

Bass Clef   Tenor Clef   Alto Clef   Treble Clef
(for soprano)

from the Latin *triplum*, which was the name given to the highest part in certain forms of medieval vocal music.

The treble and bass clefs are the ones most commonly used, mainly because these are the clefs employed in piano notation. The right hand ordinarily plays the notes on a staff with the treble clef, and the left hand plays the notes on a staff with the bass clef. A bow-shaped *brace* and a straight line placed to the left of the two staves indicate that the notes on them are to be played simultaneously, not one line first and then the next:

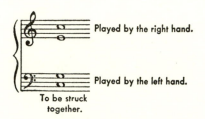

Another straight bracketlike form of the brace is used when there are three or more separate instrumental or vocal parts. Here, for example, is the way this sort of brace links together the four parts in a string quartet score:

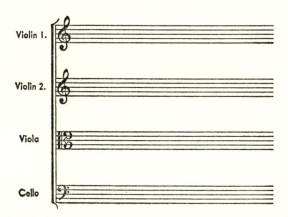

CLEF READING

A little more than a century ago the use of four different c clefs was regular practice for vocal music. Even now, if we have to consult basic editions such as the Bach Gesellschaft which use the original clefs employed by the composer, we will find not only the alto and tenor clefs but two others, now obsolete. These clefs place the staff in convenient ranges for soprano and mezzo-soprano:

Soprano Clef   Mezzo-soprano Clef

While fluency in reading these two obsolete clefs may not be absolutely essential, one should at least be able to decipher them slowly when necessary. Such is not the case, however, for the alto clef, because it is used for the notation of viola parts (see the quartet score illustration on page 24). Since the alto clef will be encountered in every string quartet or orchestral score, fluent reading of this clef is necessary for any well-trained musician. Almost equally important is the tenor clef, as it is used in standard orchestral scores for the tenor trombone (although the present tendency is to write this part in the bass clef, using many ledger lines), and also, at times, for the bassoon and cello.*

In order to insure a good start with reading staff notation, we shall treat the four clefs of modern usage with equal care at this point. This is done with the full realization that later on most practical reading will be dominated mainly by the treble and bass clefs. But the early use of the tenor and alto clefs along with the treble and bass should be beneficial to reading in general, since it will require us to read *notes* (D, E, F, etc.), and not merely staff lines and spaces. We will thereby avoid the bad habit acquired by some players of string and wind instruments—concentration on one clef at the beginning of their study causes them unconsciously to attribute pitch properties to the staff, which in itself has none. The first impression of staff notation gained here by the simultaneous use of four dif-

---

* Appendixes II and III contain further information concerning the use of various clefs by orchestral instruments.

ferent clefs must inevitably be that the staff is flexible, depending entirely on the clef signs for its meaning.

Using circular symbols, as in the previous example illustrating ledger lines, here is a chart showing the relative ranges of the four principal clefs. The range of the gamut given earlier is extended somewhat to make this possible.

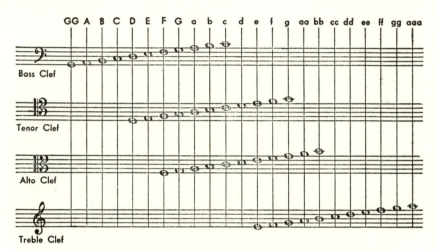

Relative Ranges of the Four Principal Clefs

STAFF-NOTATION PRACTICE

Work through the following problems; they will insure at least an initial acquaintance with the four principal clefs:

EXPERIMENT 18.

Write the following intervals in various clefs. Play them on the piano.

When writing a second, place the higher note slightly to the right. For example:

Write, play, and name the intervals:

a. *In Bass Clef*		c. *In Alto Clef*	
	A-F		G-f
	E-G		a-c
	GG-b		d-g
	B-a		b-aa
	C-d		C-e
	D-G		f-g
	F-b		g-cc
	E-e		E-b
	B-E		a-f
	D-c		F-c

b. *In Tenor Clef*		d. *In Treble Clef*	
	D-b		d-aa
	F-a		f-dd
	a-e		cc-ee
	c-f		aa-ff
	b-d		dd-gg
	a-b		e-dd
	E-c		g-aaa
	d-g		ee-gg
	F-e		bb-dd
	a-f		e-bb

EXPERIMENT 19.

a. Name these intervals as rapidly as you can. Play them at the keyboard, finding the notes as quickly as possible.

b. For dictation exercises, write similar series of intervals in various clefs. Announce the clef, give the name of one of the tones, and play at the piano. The listeners deduce the name of the other tone by identifying the interval, and write down both notes in the required clef.

c. The blackboard or a set of flash cards may be used for exercises in recognition. Intervals in various clefs may be written on the blackboard, or held up on cards for a given time (about eight counts in moderate tempo should suffice), and then removed. The group writes down the names of the tones and of the intervals, using the letters of the gamut. For example:

      A   c   e

1. D, 5   2. A, m3   3. F, M7   etc.

CHAPTER

❧4❧

Note-values

The first staff notations of pitch preceded by several centuries any similarly modern attempts at rhythmic notation. The rhythm of the earliest notated music was evidently unregulated except by tradition in singing and by the unavoidable rhythmic characteristics of the text.

As long as only a single melodic line was involved, and even when the melodic line was sung in unison by a large group, the lack of precise regulation for the time lengths was not a serious disadvantage. But when the technical development of music went beyond the early purely melodic stage, the exact lengths of the tones had to be determined and indicated in the notation. Even two singers singing different melodic lines simultaneously could not fit the tones together properly without a definite idea of the time values.

The first regulation of rhythm, however, was achieved not by an invention in notation, but by the application in performance of stereotyped rhythmical formulas—such as long-short, long-short, and so forth.* These formulas must have eventually become tiresome, and while they achieved a certain kind of rhythmic organization, they were unable, without the support of notation, to contribute to any further rhythmical development.

In the thirteenth century, overlapping the use of the formulas, rhythmic notation in the modern sense began. Two-note symbols with definite proportional time values were introduced: a "long note" (*longa*), and a "short note" (*brevis*). The long note could be divided into two or three of the short notes and the short note could be divided into two or three still shorter notes. The pos-

---

* Some of the terminology and a method of applying these formulas to melody are discussed below in Chapter 13, pp. 157–159.

sibilities of division in various sorts of proportions were explored
for a period of about a century, and by the middle of the fourteenth
century a well-developed system of rhythmical notation was in
use.

While many changes have taken place in rhythmical notation
since the fourteenth century, the principal ideas which were established by that time remain with us even today. We still rely on the
choice of a certain note-value to represent the beat, and we still have
a system which divides long notes in various ways into shorter values.

DUPLE NOTE-VALUES

The modern scale of note-values begins with the kind of open
circular note already used in the illustrations of the preceding
chapters. This note is called a *whole-note*.

The whole-note is a *duple note-value* because it divides into two
smaller notes of half its size, called *half-notes*. The half-note symbol
consists of the original *head* of the whole-note with the addition of a
stem.

The half-note continues the same process by dividing into two
quarter-notes. The quarter-note symbol has a darkened head and
a stem.

The quarter-note divides into two *eighth-notes*. The eighth-note
symbol adds one *flag* to the stem.

The eighth-note divides into two *sixteenth-notes*. The sixteenth-
note symbol has still another flag on the stem.

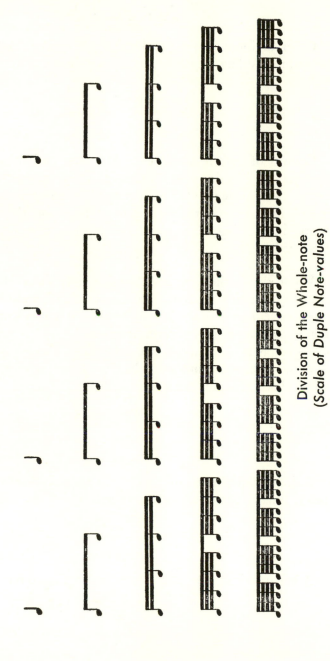

Division of the Whole-note
(Scale of Duple Note-values)

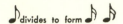 divides to form

Other divisions into successively smaller values follow the same procedure, adding a new flag for each division.

1/16   1/32   1/64   1/128

Groups of eighth-notes, sixteenth-notes, and others which use flags may be joined together by *beams*. The number of beams should be the same as the number of flags used for these notes. On page 31 is a full illustration of the division of a whole-note through the sixty-fourth-note, using beams instead of separate flags for the notes of lesser value.

While the whole-note is the longest note-value in common use, the *breve*,* which has double the length of a whole-note, may sometimes be encountered. This note-value is a survivor of medieval notation, as its name indicates. Its meaning, of course, has entirely changed, as it is not short, but quite long, according to the durations we assign to note-symbols. The breve is written in various ways, three of which are shown below:

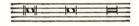

RESTS

A silence equal in duration to a whole-note is shown by an oblong mark, usually placed under the fourth line of the staff.

Whole-rest

A half-rest is usually placed on top of the third line of the staff.

Half-rest

* English form for brevis.

The *quarter-rest* has an entirely different shape,* and is usually placed in the middle of the staff.

Quarter-rest

An *eighth-rest* has a sort of flag on the left side. The number of these flags increases as the values shorten, as with notes.

⅛ ¹⁄₁₆ ¹⁄₃₂ ¹⁄₆₄ ¹⁄₁₂₈

There are no "rest-beams," but rests may be included within note-beams.

The symbol for a *breve-rest* is a thick vertical mark placed between two lines (usually the third and fourth lines).

Breve-rest

STEMS, FLAGS, AND BEAMS: NOTATION PRINCIPLES

In writing notes on the staff, stems go up when the note is below the third line, and down when they are on the third line or above.†　Ascending stems go to the right of the note-head, and descending stems to the left. But flags are always to the right.

---

* Some foreign editions use a quarter-rest which is the reverse of the eighth-rest.

⅛　¼

† This is the general rule for a single line of music on the staff. There are different rules (which need not concern us here) when two or more parts are written on one staff.

Experiment 20.

Place the stems and flags on the following notes, according to the rules given above:

When beams are used, all of the stems connected to one beam must go in the same direction. If the notes lie on both sides of the middle line, be guided by the tone farthest from the middle line in choosing the direction of the stems.

If the case is ambiguous, draw the stems down.

Notes requiring a different number of flags may still occur within one beam.

Single tones within a beam may require an extra flag. Such flags must always be inside the main beam.

EXPERIMENT 21.

Add stems and draw beams for the following groups of notes, according to the rules given above:

½ notes   ⅟₁₆ notes   ⅟₃₂ notes

Special rules determine the placement of beams in instrumental music, with legible grouping of the rhythmic patterns as the object. In reading music the eye does not single out isolated notes, but follows the page in sections, as in reading words. Proper beaming can present the eye with intelligible units which are easily followed, while poor beaming can cause much difficulty in reading.

In vocal music legibility of the rhythmic patterns is not usually the primary consideration; beams are used to show the groups of notes which are to be sung on one syllable. Notes to which separate syllables are sung have separate flags. (A recent tendency, however, has been to treat vocal notation in the same way as instrumental notation, using beams for purposes of rhythmic legibility rather than relating them to the words.)

Specific rules for beaming in instrumental music will be introduced from time to time as needed in this chapter, and will be discussed further in Chapters 5, 6, 7, and 8. The traditional rules for beaming in vocal music will be discussed in Chapter 13.

TRIPLE NOTE-VALUES: THE AUGMENTATION DOT

All the notes in the scale of duple note-values divide into two notes of the next smaller size. While we have no "scale of triple note-values," we can make any one of the originally duple notes equal to three of the next smaller size by adding to it an *augmentation dot*.* The dot increases the value of any note to which it is added by one half. For example:

* The breve is the only exception; it is never dotted.

♩ equals ♪ ♪ but ♩. equals ♪ ♪ ♪

The same procedure applies to rests.

𝄾 equals 𝄿 𝄿 but 𝄾· equals 𝄿 𝄿 𝄿

A second dot affects the first dot as the first dot affected the note —it adds half value. A note or rest with a *double dot* has altogether three fourths added to its original length.

♩. equals ♪ ♪ ♪ but ♩.. equals ♪ ♪ ♪ ♪

METRIC UNITS: THE RELATIVITY OF NOTE-VALUES

In order to notate rhythmic patterns we must choose one note-value to represent the tones which move at the speed of the beat. This note-value is called the *metric unit*, since it is the one by which the others are measured. Tones moving faster than the beat (divisions) will be shown by note-values shorter than the one chosen as the metric unit, while tones moving more slowly than the beat (multiplications) will be shown by note-values that are longer than the metric unit.

The choice of a metric unit depends upon the rhythmic character of the music in question. In general, it is best for clear reading to choose a unit which will not result in a page full of confusing black beams. At the other extreme, it is best not to choose a unit which will result in too many large values requiring no beams at all, thereby losing the advantages of beamed groupings. In neither case will the music sound any different; it will just look different.

Except in relation to a given metric unit, note-values have no qualities of "fast" or "slow." A value like the sixteenth-note may conceivably be the metric unit of a piece in which the beat is only 40 on the metronome. There would be, then, only 40 sixteenth-notes in a whole minute. On the other hand, a value like the half-note may be the metric unit of a piece in which the beat moves at 152 on the metronome. In this case there would be 152 half-notes within one minute.

The three most commonly used metric units from the duple note-value scale given earlier are the quarter-note, the half-note, and the eighth-note, with the quarter-note unit being used about as much in standard practice as the other two combined. Just as we treated the four commonest clefs equally, even though the treble and bass clefs predominate in ordinary usage, we shall treat the commonest metric units equally here, in spite of the predominance of the quarter-note unit.

In the same category as the inability to read more than two clefs, fostered by the predominance of the treble and bass clefs, is the fixed idea that "a quarter-note gets a beat," which is fostered by the predominance of this one unit.* The policy adopted here of avoiding undue emphasis on one unit parallels the policy adopted in regard to clef reading; it tries to develop true reading, which in the case of rhythm involves rapid analysis of the *relative* values of the notes. This is best accomplished by the use of a variety of metric units. Common practice notwithstanding, the student who learns to read rhythms according to a broader approach at the start will have an advantage in his studies over the student who faces these problems only later, and with certain stubbornly fixed notions resulting from a too limited early approach.

The three commonest duple metric units are shown in a diagram (page 38) which is also intended to show the flexibility of the note-symbols. A sixteenth-note, for example, functions in one case as a third-division note, in another as a second-division note, and in still another as a first-division note, according to the metric unit employed. The diagram is limited merely for convenience to note-values ranging from the sixteenth-note through the whole-note.

A dotted note may serve as a *triple metric unit*. The three commonest triple metric units are the *dotted quarter-note*, the *dotted eighth-note*, and the *dotted half-note*, with the dotted quarter-note being used much more often than the others.

When a triple unit is used, the first division will consist of three undotted notes of the next smaller value. For example, if the unit is

---

* Choral directors know only too well how firmly fixed this idea is among amateurs. Much old choral music (Palestrina, etc.) is printed in modern editions which use the half-note as the metric unit. Singers have great difficulty in escaping the idea that these are "slow notes."

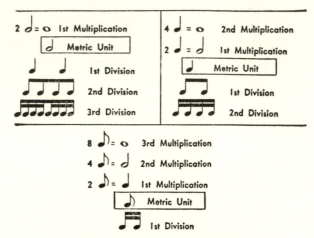

The Three Commonest Duple Units

a dotted quarter-note, the first division will consist of three eighth-notes.

After this, since we do not have a real triple series, all other divisions are duple. The three notes of the first division divide by twos into six second-division notes, the six notes of the second division divide into twelve third-division notes, and so forth.

The multiplications of a triple unit are dotted notes of twice, four times, eight times, etc., the value of the unit. The multiplications of triple units, therefore, grow according to the duple series. (The absence of a real triple series in our notation means that we have no single note-value which will be three times, six times, or nine times, etc., the length of a given triple unit.)

Here is a diagram showing the three principal triple units with some of their divisions and multiplications:

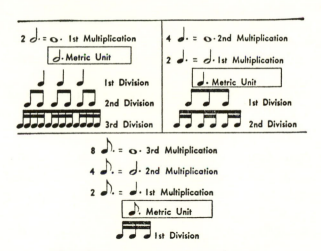

The Three Commonest Triple Units

RHYTHMIC-NOTATION PRACTICE

Even the most gifted student at some point in his training has to come face to face with the arithmetic of note-values. There is, however, something innately contradictory for him about this situation; music is a thing he "feels," and having to perform any action resembling arithmetical calculation seems to him to violate music's nature. And yet, without perfect clearness on the question of note-values he cannot satisfactorily bring music from the page into sound. Singers, whose feeling about the production of musical sounds is the most natural one, seem to resist an orderly treatment of rhythmic values even more than instrumentalists. But in any case, every good musician, whatever his medium, is severely handicapped if he is slow in grasping rhythmical structures as they appear on the page. If he is not an accurate and fast reader his only learning process must be that of imitation and rote; he is in the position of an illiterate person whose only source of information is what other people tell him.

To provide practice material consolidating the information just given about note-values, and to make certain that the hypothetical student who is learning everything here for the first time does not turn out later to be an arithmetically confused performer, we shall perform some experiments in writing rhythms. We shall transcribe the patterns used for rhythmic tapping in Chapter 2 into real musical notation.

The patterns of Chapter 2 were divisions of beats into two, four, and six parts. If we look at the two charts showing divisions of various metric units (pages 38 and 39), we see that:

1. Patterns of two occur as first-division notes of duple units. Therefore, the rudimentary notation | | may be expressed as ♫ with a quarter-note unit, as ♩ ♩ with a half-note unit, and as ♫ with an eighth-note unit.

2. Patterns of four occur as second-division notes of duple units. Therefore, the rudimentary notation | | | | may be expressed as

3. Patterns of six occur as second-division notes of triple units. Therefore, the rudimentary notation | | | | | | may be expressed

In the earlier rhythmic exercises we concerned ourselves with patterns defined only by points of attack, expressed by tapping. But if we were to sing these patterns, we would have to show not only where the notes are attacked, but exactly how long they are sustained. For example, the rudimentary pattern | | - | may be sung in two ways: the third fraction of the beat (represented by the dash) can be a real silence, or the sound of the second fraction may be sustained *through* the third fraction. The difference between these two versions would not be one of pattern, as this is defined by the beginnings of the notes, but simply one of articulation. If the third fraction is to be silent, a rest must be used in real musical notation, and if not, one longer tone must fill the space of both the second and third fractions. These two possible versions would be shown in musical notation as follows:

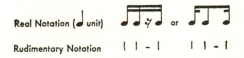

In transcribing the rudimentary patterns of Chapter 2, we shall include variants of this kind, and in the ear-training exercises to be performed after the transcription we shall learn to listen carefully for these small distinctions. A meticulous musician is always very careful about such matters. Although he may not be at all literal in reproducing what he sees on the page, he treats the composer's notation freely as a matter of taste and choice, not merely through carelessness or inability to read precisely.

The line and dash notation employed earlier had no meaning in real musical notation. It was simply a device which served a useful purpose at the time, and it is to be discarded now for another such device which will serve as a final bridge to real musical notation. In order that we may give the exact lengths of the tones in the various patterns, including the variants, we shall show the patterns here in terms of numerical fractions. *The fractions represent the exact amount of the beat occupied by the tones.* For example, the pattern I I divides the beat into halves. This pattern, then, would be shown in fractions as ½ ½. If a rest were involved, the fraction would be placed in parentheses. The pattern I I - I, using a rest for the third fraction, would be ¼ ¼ (¼) ¼. If a rest were not used, and the second and third fractions were to be shown by one note of longer value, the pattern would be given in fractions as ¼ ½ ¼.

These fractions are not to be confused with note-values. Only after a note-value is chosen for the metric unit can note-values be assigned to the fractions. This is one of the advantages of the use of fractions here; all rhythms can be shown independently of the metric unit. One fraction, therefore, can represent three or more different musical notations.

The number of fractions on the following pages, and the realization that there would be at least three times as many more groups in musical notation, may present a somewhat forbidding aspect! The intention, however, is not to insist on the full working out of each fraction given, in all variants, and with each metric unit. The lists of fractions, as representations of the possible permutations of the patterns of two, four and six given in Chapter 2, are complete. But it can be decided in individual cases whether it is necessary to do only a small part, a large part, or all of them. After a sampling of each of the various groups, this decision can easily be made.

A key to the fractions when a duple metric unit is used would read as follows:

½ is a note of the first division.

¾ is a note of the first division with a dot.

¼ is a note of the second division.

⅛ is a note of the third division.

⅞ is a note of the first division with a double dot.

(If the fraction is enclosed by a parenthesis a rest is indicated.)

EXPERIMENT 22.

Write out the following rhythmic patterns—first with a quarter-note unit, then with eighth- and half-note units. In every case in which it is possible, include the whole group under one beam.

Practice singing the patterns on "la" while clapping the beats with your hands.

First Division   (These patterns are the same ones given in Experiment 17.)

½	½
½	(½)
(½)	½

Second Division   Two different articulations are given for some patterns. (These patterns, also, were given in Experiment 17.)

¼	¼	¼	¼				
½	¼	¼	or	¼	(¼)	¼	¼
¼	¼	½	or	¼	¼	¼	(¼)
¼	(¼)	¼	(¼)				
(¼)	¼	¼	¼				
¼	½	¼	or	¼	¼	(¼)	¼
(½)	¼	¼					
(¼)	¼	(¼)	¼	or	(¼)	½	¼
¼	(¼)	(¼)	¼	or	½	(¼)	¼
¾	¼						
(¼)	¼	(½)					
(¼)	½	¼					
¼	¾						
(½)	¼	(¼)					
(¾)	¼						

Third Division   Carry the top beam over the whole group, but for greater legibility with the large patterns carry the others through only half of the group. For example:

⅛	⅛	⅛	⅛	⅛	⅛	⅛	⅛
¼	⅛	⅛	⅛	⅛	¼		
⅞	⅛						
⅛	¼	⅛	⅛	¼	⅛		

The divisions of a triple unit produce an almost fantastic number of patterns. Here we shall work with only the first and second divisions. But even these, with different articulations, exceed a hundred.

Here is a key to the fractions when triple metric units are used:

⅓ is a note of the first division.

⅙ is a note of the second division.

3/6 is a note of the first division with a dot.

⅔ is a note twice the length of the first division.

No single note can have the quantity of ⅚ which is sometimes called for in these patterns. It is produced by linking two other fractions by a curved line called a *tie*. Ties are placed next to the noteheads.

⅔ + ⅙ = ⅚ or (♩. Unit)

⅙ + ⅔ = ⅚ or (𝅗𝅥. Unit)

EXPERIMENT 23.

Work out the following patterns derived from triple units, and perform them, as before.

First Division Notate these patterns with each of the three main triple units (♪., ♩., and 𝅗𝅥.). (These patterns were given in Experiment 17.)

⅓	⅓	⅓	⅓	⅔	
⅓	(⅓)	⅓	⅓	(⅓)	(⅓)
⅔	⅓		(⅓)	⅓	⅓
⅓	⅓	(⅓)	(⅓)	⅓	(⅓)

(⅓) ⅔
(⅓) (⅓) ⅓ [(⅔) ⅓ is a less common form]

The number six can be divided by two or by three. So, likewise, can patterns of six notes be grouped in two different ways: they may consist of two groups of three notes, or three groups of two notes. Good notation can show by the use of beams which kind of grouping is intended.

With single beams (eighth-notes) six notes may be shown as:

With two or three beams (sixteenth- or thirty-second-notes) the upper beam can span the whole pattern, and the lower beam can show the grouping.

Even complex patterns should show their origins from 2 × 3, or 3 × 2. The pattern 2/6 1/6 1/6 2/6, for example, can be grouped in the following ways, according to its origin:

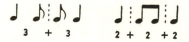

The disassociation of the two middle notes in the first case by the use of separate flags shows that each of them belongs to a different section of the pattern, while joining them in the second case shows that they belong to the same section of the pattern. This is our first application of an important notation principle: *use beams to join rhythmical fragments which are to be grouped together*, and conversely, *do not cross with beams rhythmical fragments which are to be perceived separately*.

Sometimes in carrying out the principle of preserving the appearance of basic groupings certain tones may have to be divided, placing half of them in one section of the pattern and the other half in another section. In such cases, the two parts of the tone are linked together by a tie. Here is an example in which only the use of a tie can make possible a literal representation of the grouping 2 + 2 + 2:

In spite of the above principle, however, patterns with the basic scheme 2 + 2 + 2 need not always be shown in three sections. They can, without destroying their nature, also be shown in groupings of 2 + 4 or 4 + 2. For example, the pattern just illustrated above could be written just as clearly in the following way:

However, to show the pattern in a manner which suggests 3 + 3 would imply the rival grouping, and would violate its nature:

The patterns of the following experiment are second divisions of triple units. This means that they were formed by dividing into twos the three notes of the first division of a triple metric unit.

Triple Metric Unit

First Division

Second Division

The essential grouping of these patterns, then, is 2 + 2 + 2, and their notation should use beams in a manner which makes this grouping clear. We shall have occasion later on to use the grouping 3 + 3. In this experiment, however, any beaming which implies this grouping should be avoided.

EXPERIMENT 24.

Work out the following patterns of six as second divisions of triple units. Use each of the commonest units (♪., ♩. and ♩.). (These patterns, too, were given in Experiment 17.)

```
⅙  ⅙  ⅙  ⅙  ⅙  ⅙

²⁄₆ ⅙  ⅙  ⅙  ⅙       or  ⅙ (⅙) ⅙  ⅙  ⅙  ⅙

⅙  ⅙  ⅓  ⅙  ⅙       or  ⅙  ⅙  ⅙ (⅙) (⅙) ⅙

⅙  ⅙  ⅙  ⅙  ⅓       or  ⅙  ⅙  ⅙  ⅙  ⅙ (⅙)

⅙  ³⁄₆ ⅙  ⅙          or  ⅙  ⅓ (⅙) ⅙  ⅙
                     or  ⅙  ⅙ (⅓) ⅙  ⅙

⅙  ⅙  ⅙  ⅙ (⅓)      or  ⅙  ⅙  ⅙  ⅓ (⅙)
                     or  ⅙  ⅙  ⅙  ³⁄₆

⅓  ⅓  ⅙  ⅙          or  ⅙ (⅙) ⅙ (⅙) ⅙  ⅙
                     or  ⅙ (⅙) ⅓  ⅙  ⅙
                     or  ⅓  ⅙ (⅙) ⅙  ⅙

⅓  ⅙  ⅙  ⅓          or  ⅙ (⅙) ⅙  ⅙  ⅓
                     or  ⅙ (⅙) ⅙  ⅙  ⅙ (⅙)
                     or  ⅓  ⅙  ⅙  ⅙ (⅙)
```

1/6 (1/6) 1/6 (1/6) 1/6 (1/6)   or   1/6 (1/6) 1/3 1/3
                              or   1/3 1/6 (1/6) 1/6 (1/6)
                              or   1/3 1/3 1/6 (1/6)

1/3 1/6 3/6   or   1/6 (1/6) 1/6 3/6
                or   1/6 (1/6) 1/6 1/3 1/6
                or   1/3 1/6 1/6 (1/3)

1/6 3/6 1/3   or   1/6 1/3 (1/6) 1/3
                or   1/6 1/6 (1/3) 1/6 (1/6)
                or   1/6 1/6 (1/3) 1/3

1/6 5/6 (write as 1/6 1/6‿2/3)   or   1/6 1/6 (1/3) (1/3)
                                      or   1/6 1/6 1/6‿(3/6)

(1/6) 1/6 1/6 1/6 1/6 1/6
1/6 1/3 1/6 1/6 1/6   or   1/6 1/6 (1/6) 1/6 1/6 1/6
1/6 1/6 1/6 1/3 1/6   or   1/6 1/6 1/6 1/6 (1/6) 1/6
1/6 1/6 3/6 1/6   or   1/6 1/6 1/3 (1/6) 1/6
                   or   1/6 1/6 1/6 (1/3) 1/6

(1/3) 1/6 1/6 1/6 1/6
1/3 1/6 1/3 1/6   or   1/6 (1/6) 1/6 1/3 1/6
                   or   1/3 1/6 1/6 (1/6) 1/6

1/6 1/3 1/3 1/6   or   1/6 1/6 (1/6) 1/3 1/6
                   or   1/6 1/6 (1/6) 1/6 (1/6) 1/6

(1/6) 1/6 1/6 1/3 1/6   or   (1/6) 1/6 1/6 1/6 (1/6) 1/6
(3/6) 1/6 1/6 1/6
1/6 2/3 1/6   or   1/6 3/6 (1/6) 1/6
            or   1/6 1/3 (1/3) 1/6

(1/6) 1/6 (1/6) 1/6 (1/6) 1/6   or   (1/6) 1/3 1/3 1/6
                               or   (1/6) 1/6 (1/6) 1/3 1/6

(1/6) 1/6 1/3 1/3   or   (1/6) 1/6 1/6 (1/6) 1/3
                   or   (1/6) 1/6 1/6 (1/6) 1/6 (1/6)

(1/6) 1/3 1/6 1/6 (1/6)   or   (1/6) 1/6 (1/6) 1/6 1/3
1/6 2/3 1/6   [More of the feeling that this pattern derives
from a group of six is preserved by this notation, which uses a tie:
1/6   1/6   3/6‿ 1/6]

(1/3) 3/6 1/6 or (1/3) 1/3 (1/6) 1/6
or 1/3 1/6 (1/3) 1/6
(3/6) 1/3 1/6 or (3/6) 1/6 (1/6) 1/6
5/6 1/6 [write as 2/3 1/6 1/6] or 2/3 (1/6) 1/6
or 3/6 (1/3) 1/6 or 1/3 (3/6) 1/6
or 1/6 (1/3) (1/3) 1/6
(1/6) 5/6 [write (1/6) 1/6 2/3] or (1/6) 2/3 (1/6)
or (1/6) 3/6 (1/3) or (1/6) 1/3 (3/6)
or (1/6) 1/6 (2/3)
(3/6) 3/6 or (3/6) 1/3 (1/6) or (3/6) 1/6 (1/3)
(2/3) 1/3 or (2/3) 1/6 (1/6)
(5/6) 1/6 [write (1/3) (3/6) 1/6, since the rests cannot be tied.]

Using the patterns worked out in the above experiments, try dictation exercises. The performer announces the metric unit, then sings the pattern, clapping the beats. The listeners take them down as follows, showing the unit and one beat of the pattern.

Here are examples. All these patterns are derived from the fractions in Experiments 22, 23, and 24.

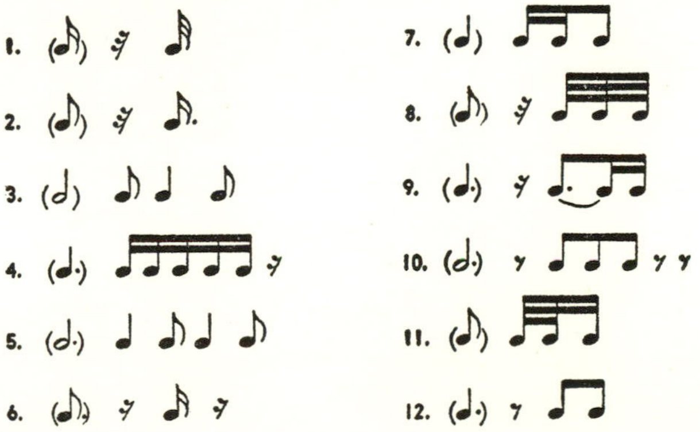

13.

14.

15.

16.

17.

18.

19.

20.

CHAPTER

🙚5🙚

Meters

In learning to execute the various patterns resulting from division we put together long sequences of beats. In our concentration on the divisions we made no attempt to group the beats themselves into rhythmic patterns. If we had not been so preoccupied, we probably would have thought of this stream of beats in groups of two or three. The first beat in each group would have been defined by an *accent* (sign: >; in some editions: ∧).

ACCENT

The most general definition of an accent would state that it is *an emphasis of any kind that lends prominence to a given point in time*. Such emphases may come from three sources:

1. From the mind (*psychological accent*)—we impose this emphasis ourselves by directing more attention to a certain point.
2. From the rhythmic structure (*agogic accent*)—a tone which is of greater length than its neighbors gains emphasis.
3. From extrarhythmical sources (*dynamic accent*)—a tone which is louder, or in some other way more conspicuous in sound than its neighbors, will gain emphasis.

Psychological accents can be demonstrated by means of simple experiments:

EXPERIMENT 25.

a. A performer taps with some object, producing a stream of beats of equal length and loudness. He thinks of groups of two or three

51

as he taps, but avoids any audible indication of his thoughts. He then asks several listeners what groupings they have heard. The answers will seldom coincide with the tapper's thoughts, nor will they show any degree of consistency among the listeners.

b. A similar experiment may be performed by listening to the ticking of an electric metronome, which produces sounds of perfect evenness. If the attention is held forcibly on the ticking, the feeling of some kind of grouping will arise automatically, as it is either against human nature or against our habits of thought to perceive long streams of beats without segmentation. Among the listeners there will be a variety of impressions, because these impressions are in the minds of the hearers, not in the sounds.

Since there seems to be a human predisposition to hear tones in groups of some kind rather than in one long undefined stream, the other kinds of accents which originate externally have the function of satisfying the mind's need for definition, while preventing it from choosing completely arbitrary groupings which would differ with each listener.

The second kind of accent, agogic accent, is the true rhythmical accent. The greater length of some tones directs the attention normally to these points, leaving no room for imagined accents such as those observed in the above experiment.

Experiment 26.

Sing with "la" the following rhythmical sequence, making the sound as even in volume as possible. Note the stresses which can be felt on the longer tones.

Agogic accents can be added in performance to notes which are written with even values. In fact, agogic accents are the best means of relieving the monotony of long successions of even notes, and of making clear the groupings intended. Agogic accents not contained in the note-values themselves are very short lengthenings of the tones, and they can be shown by dashes placed next to the noteheads, called *tenuto* marks (Italian: *tenare*, to hold).

Experiment 27.

Sing the following succession of tones, slightly lengthening those which have tenuto marks:

The agogic accent is of particular importance for instruments such as the organ or harpsichord which cannot make individual notes louder than the others around them (dynamic accent). While absolutely vital to the harpsichord and the organ, agogic accents are not less important for string instruments, wind instruments, or even singing, since they can contribute so much to the clarity of rhythmical articulation. In combination with dynamic stress, agogic accents gain an even higher degree of expressiveness. On instruments which have the possibility of both dynamic and agogic accents, these two kinds of accents are often used in combination.

The third kind of accent, dynamic accent, is the least subtle of the three types. Having no intrinsic rhythmical power, it gains its way through loudness and excess energy. If overdone or misplaced, dynamic accents can be very obtrusive in the flow of a musical line. The force of this kind of accent is such that it is even able to overthrow an agogic accent. For example, the pattern "short-long" will have its stress on the second tone, on the basis of agogic accent. By means of a strong dynamic accent this impression may be reversed.

When this pattern is sung with even volume, the accent will be heard on the longer tone.

When this pattern is sung with strong dynamic emphasis on the shorter tone, that note becomes the accented one.

Other factors besides loudness may account for accents which belong in an indirect way to the third category. For instance, a peak note in a melodic line may be heard as accented, provided all other factors are equal.

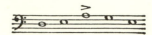

Accents may also be felt through the influence of chords which are in some way more conspicuous than the other chords around them. Even a factor such as tone color (not loudness, but a brighter quality of sound) may lend prominence to certain tones, producing the impression of accents.

Major parts of the performer's art are the proper placement of the kinds of accents which he can add to the music, and a proper sensitivity to the other kinds which are already present, but which must be reduced or emphasized in the interest of a balanced projection of the musical line.

METER

When two or more groups of beats with similarly placed accents follow each other, a *meter* is established. In the following rhythmical succession, for example, agogic accents make clear a regular distribution of the beats in patterns of three, with the quarter-note as the metric unit.

Meters are indicated in notation by signs placed at the beginning of the piece (or at other points if the meter changes). The signs are called *time signatures,* and they consist of two numbers, one placed over the other. For example:

$$\frac{3}{4} \qquad \frac{4}{4}$$

If the metric unit is duple (an undotted note), *the upper number tells the number of beats within a metric group and the lower number indicates the note value which represents the beat.*

In the time signature $\frac{3}{4}$, then, the 3 means three beats in the metric group, and the 4 means a quarter-note gets a beat.

The metric groups, to which we refer as *measures* or *bars,* are separated in the music by vertical lines drawn through the staff called *bar-lines* or *measure-lines. Double-bars* are used in endings. At the ends of sections two thin lines are used. At the ends of whole pieces the second line is thickened.

Bar- or Measure-line   Sectional Double-bar   Final Double-bar

The rhythmic example given above (page 54) had three beats within each metric group, or bar, and these beats were represented by a quarter-note metric unit. The time signature for that example, then, would be $\frac{3}{4}$, derived according to the procedure outlined above. Here is the same example shown in full musical notation:

Once an order of accents has been established, as expressed by a certain meter, we begin to expect their recurrence. They produce a form of psychological accent, called *metric accent.*

If a dynamic or agogic accent coincides with the expected metric accent, we classify it as a *regular accent.* If it conflicts with the metric accent, it is an *irregular accent.*

Conflict between the metric accents which are expected and the other kinds which are unpredictable forms one of the most important sources for rhythmic tension and interest. For instance, if the example of $\frac{3}{4}$ meter given above is performed with a regular dynamic accent coinciding with the already too clearly expressed metrical accents on the first beats of each bar, the result is an even more obvious and dull rhythmic structure than before. But if it is performed with dynamic accents in irregular places, as indicated below, it gains new and unexpected interest:

If the same rhythmic quantities as shown above, with the agogic accents they imply, were placed in opposition to the expected metric accents of $\frac{3}{4}$ meter, still greater tension would be created. Here is the same rhythmic sequence shifted over by two quarters so that it conflicts with the meter rather than supports it:

We shall discuss the kind of rhythmic situation created by this device later in the chapter on syncopation (Chapter 7). The important fact it reveals here is that meter and rhythm may be placed in conflict with each other. While in simple music the various forms of accent combine to support the meter, in more sophisticated styles the accents are opposed to each other in endlessly varied combinations. The meter in such complex cases is mainly a device to assist the performer in executing the free rhythmic groups formed through irregular stresses. The meter exists *behind* the music, like a piece of graph paper placed behind an object simply as a means of judging its proportions.

SIMPLE METERS, CONDUCTING PATTERNS

Meters which use duple metric units are called *simple meters*. Here are two-measure examples of various simple meters:

The accent marks in the above example indicate the *primary metric accents*. The marks in parentheses indicate *secondary metric accents*. Secondary accents occur in all meters which are multiples or combinations of two or three.

The time signatures $\frac{2}{2}$ and $\frac{4}{4}$ are sometimes indicated by the signs

¢ and C. These symbols, which look like the letter C, are actually half-circles. They descend from the system of rhythmic notation in use before 1600, when *tempus perfectum* (triple division of the brevis) was indicated by a circle, and *tempus imperfectum* (duple division) was indicated by a half-circle.

A feeling for the various meters can be strengthened by practicing the patterns used in conducting them. The conducting pattern for a bar of two beats (whatever the metric unit may be) is:

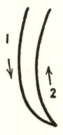

Two Beats

The conducting pattern for a bar of three beats (whatever the metric unit may be) is:

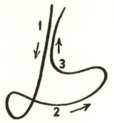

Three Beats

The conducting pattern for a bar of four beats (whatever the metric unit may be) is:

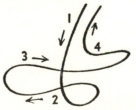

Four Beats

In simple meters at very slow tempos (50 or less), the first division may be felt as the beat more easily than the original unit. Slow measures of this kind may be subdivided by the insertion of "and" between the counts. For example:

In conducting divided beats, the "ands" are represented by loops inserted into the regular beat forms. Here are conducting patterns for divided beats of two, three, and four:

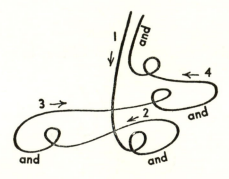

Divided Two

Divided Three

Divided Four

COMPOUND METERS, CONDUCTING PATTERNS

A different method is necessary in deriving the time signatures for meters in which the beat is represented by triple units (dotted notes). Two dotted quarter-notes in a measure would have to be shown as follows by the former method:

$$\frac{2}{\frac{1}{4} + \frac{1}{8}}$$

This method is unquestionably clumsy, and the substitute for it which we must by convention employ is almost as bad. The rule is that the *upper figure shows the number of first-division notes in a bar, and the lower number tells what these first-division notes are.*

Two ♩. in a bar means that there are six ♪ in a bar. Therefore, the time signature will be $\frac{6}{8}$. Here is a short example:

Meters which use triple units are called *compound meters*. Here are examples of compound meters:

When the tempo is moderate or fast, compound meters are conducted in the same manner as simple meters. Bars with six first-division notes are conducted in two, bars with nine first-division notes
in three, and bars with twelve first-division notes in four. But in
very slow tempos compound meters may be regulated more easily
by the first divisions than by the original dotted units. For example,
if a $\frac{6}{8}$ meter moves at 40 to the $\downarrow$., we may feel the pulse more easily
if we count the first-division eighth-notes as beats which move at
120. In many instances compound meters lie just at the dividing point
between our feeling for fast and slow. In these instances we are able
to feel simultaneously the rocking rhythm of the slow unit and the
flow of the fast unit (for example, a tempo of about 50 to the $\downarrow$. and
150 to the $\downarrow$). The designation "compound" is particularly appropriate to these meters at the tempos which divide our attention between triple units and their first divisions, and they are conducted
so that both rhythmic levels are visible. In bars of nine and twelve
slow beats, the basic forms of the beats for measures of three and
four are retained, with two additional loops inserted between each
of the main beats to represent the first-division notes. Here are diagrams of the conducting patterns for measures with nine and twelve
beats:

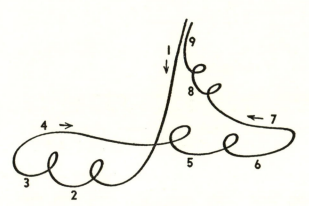

Nine Beats

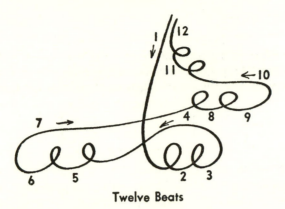

Twelve Beats

Bars with six slow beats, however, are not quite simply bars of two beats with loops inserted. There are two standard forms for conducting this kind of measure. The Italian form bears the closest resemblance to the basic two-beat, as its "four" (which is the secondary accent) swings to the left. In the German form the "four" swings to the right, which is the reverse of the direction taken by "two" in a two-beat measure. Here are diagrams of the two kinds of conducting patterns for measures with six slow beats:

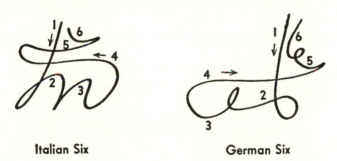

Italian Six   **German Six**

RHYTHMIC-NOTATION PRACTICE

We can extract still more value from the rhythmic patterns shown in fractions on pages 43 through 49 by transcribing them as complete measures, employing various time signatures. For example, the pattern ½ ¼ ¼ could be writen as a whole bar of two beats or four beats.

EXPERIMENT 28.

Write some of the patterns of two and four given as fractions in Experiment 22, pages 43 and 44, so that each pattern fills a complete measure. Use the following time signatures for these measures:

$$\frac{2}{8} \quad \frac{2}{4} \quad \frac{2}{2} \quad \frac{4}{8} \quad \frac{4}{4} \quad \frac{4}{2}$$

The notation of rhythms written within bars of four beats brings up problems of legibility similar to those encountered in notating patterns of six notes. The problem in measures of four beats is to preserve the grouping into two sections of two beats each, defined by the primary and secondary accents. The position of the secondary accent (the third beat) should always be visible. Neither beams nor rests should span the secondary accent, although long notes frequently do. For example:

EXPERIMENT 29.

a. Write some of the patterns of three, given as fractions in Experiment 23, page 44, so that each pattern fills a complete measure. Use the following time signatures for these measures:

$$\frac{3}{8} \quad \frac{3}{4} \quad \frac{3}{2} \quad \frac{9}{8} \quad \frac{9}{4} \quad \frac{9}{2}$$

b. Write some of the patterns of six, given in fractions in Experiment 24, pages 47 through 49, to fill out complete measures employing the following time signatures:

$$\frac{3}{8} \quad \frac{3}{4} \quad \frac{3}{2}$$

The bars using triple units (♪., ♩. and 𝅗𝅥.) may be filled out with first-division notes by adding together patterns of three in various combinations. For example:

EXPERIMENT 30.

Use two or more of the patterns of three given in fractions in Experiment 23, page 44, to fill out complete measures employing the following time signatures:

$$\frac{6}{16} \quad \frac{6}{8} \quad \frac{6}{4} \quad \frac{9}{16} \quad \frac{9}{8} \quad \frac{9}{4} \quad \frac{12}{16} \quad \frac{12}{8} \quad \frac{12}{4}$$

Bars using triple units present certain problems of notation. To insure legibility, the secondary accents in these bars should be plainly discernible. For example, the middle of a $\frac{6}{8}$ bar should not be spanned by a beam, single note-value, or rest (except for a whole-rest, or a note which by itself fills out the entire measure).

The secondary accents are concealed in the above example, and the duple groupings suggest $\frac{3}{4}$. Here are correct forms:

An exception to the rule that $\frac{3}{4}$ and $\frac{6}{8}$ should be notated differently is the following pattern, which is commonly used:

The first notation has the appearance of a $\frac{6}{8}$ grouping, but it destroys no secondary accent, since there is none in $\frac{3}{4}$.

Another convention of notation requires that a rest of ⅔ of a triple unit use two ⅓ rests rather than a single large rest, unless the ⅔ rest falls on the accent. For example:

IRREGULAR METERS, CONDUCTING PATTERNS

The basic groups of two and three combine to produce *irregular meters*, such as those consisting of five or seven beats to a measure. The distribution of the secondary accents in these irregular measures varies. For example:

Bars with five beats in fast tempo may be conducted with asymmetrical two-beats, making the "three" portion of the measure longer than the "two" portion.

In slow tempo, bars of five may be conducted by combinations of the two-beat and the three-beat. In using these beat forms, the first beat of the measure must be distinctly larger than the other downbeat which marks the point of the secondary accent. Here are five-beats formed by combining the two simpler beats of two and three:

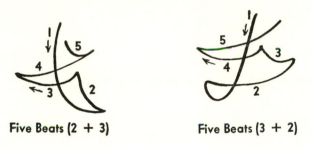

Five Beats (2 + 3)   Five Beats (3 + 2)

A slow measure of 3 + 2 may also be conducted as a shortened form of the Italian six-beat. This is the clearest form for 3 + 2, as the secondary accent is fully visible, but cannot be confused with the first beat of the measure.

Five Beats (3 + 2 as a shortened six)

Bars of seven in fast tempo may be conducted by asymmetrical three-beats, giving one beat of the proper length to each of the three sections of the measure, as defined by the secondary accents.

In slow tempo, bars of seven may add loops to the form of the three-beat (as in the case of the nine-beat). One loop is added for each section of the bar containing two beats, and two loops are added to the section containing three beats. Here are some forms of the slow seven-beat:

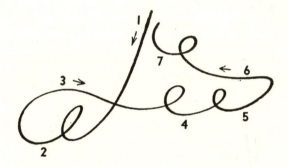

Seven Beats (2 + 3 + 2)

Seven Beats (3 + 2 + 2)

Rarely one may encounter bars of ten, eleven, thirteen, or fourteen, which are produced by the combination of groups of four and three. For example:

In fast tempos (usually the case with such measures) these bars may be conducted with asymmetrical forms of the simpler beats, which indicate the sections of the measure.

In slow tempos these meters may be conducted by adding or subtracting loops from the nine- or twelve-beat patterns. Here are some examples of this procedure:

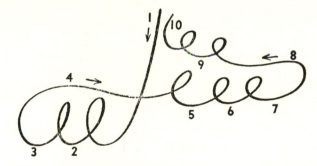

Ten Beats (3 + 4 + 3)

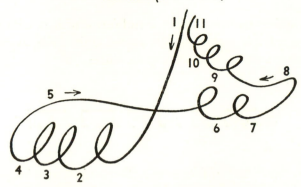

Eleven Beats (4 + 3 + 4)

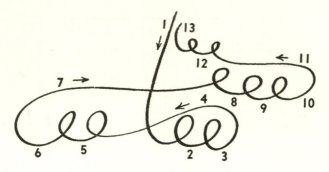

Thirteen Beats (3 + 3 + 4 + 3)

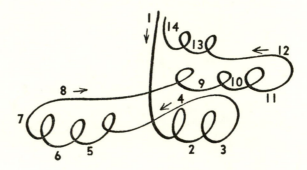

Fourteen Beats (3 + 4 + 4 + 3)

Bars of fifteen are usually compound forms of bars with five beats (i.e., using a triple rather than a dotted unit). For example, five dotted quarters give the following measure:

In fast tempo a bar of fifteen may be conducted with one of the forms of the five-beat. But in slow tempo loops have to be added, producing very complex beat patterns such as the one below:

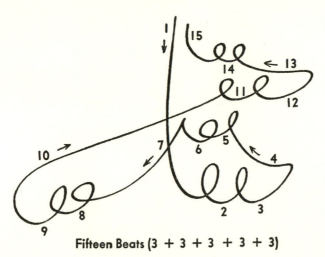

Fifteen Beats (3 + 3 + 3 + 3 + 3)

There are some instances in standard literature of the consistent use of an irregular meter throughout a whole piece. But in most instances (mainly in contemporary music) the irregular meters are mixed with regular ones, the whole point in using them being to escape any sort of too regularly recurring metric accents.

Using the patterns worked out as full measures in Experiments 28, 29, and 30, try dictation exercises. Also write and use for dictation some examples of irregular measures. The performer announces the time signature, then taps or plays the measure a number of times in succession, counting the beats aloud. More exact articulations may be shown by singing the measures and tapping the beats.

CHAPTER
✻6✻
Foreign Patterns

Very often, even in simple music, a group of tones occurs which does not conform to the prevailing type of division or multiplication. For instance, we may require three notes to occupy the space of a duple unit such as a quarter-note. Just because of this one pattern it would not be worthwhile to change the metric unit to a dotted quarter-note, and the meter to $\frac{6}{8}$. There is a method of isolating and defining such *foreign patterns* without changing the unit or meter. A number telling how many notes are in the pattern is placed next to the beam enclosing the pattern, or, if no beam is used, a bracket is added, and the number is placed in the bracket.

When the beams themselves make the grouping of the foreign patterns clear, it is unnecessary to repeat the number over and over with each occurrence of the pattern.

The note-values used for foreign patterns are the smallest ones which, when added together, exceed the amount of time supposed to be occupied by the pattern. For example, if three notes must occupy the space of a quarter-note, eighth-notes must be used, as three of them just exceed a quarter, while three sixteenth-notes would fall short.

The function of the number, or the number and bracket, then, is always to *contract* the values of the notes used, not to expand them. A duple pattern may occur where three notes are in order.

Perhaps the most commonly encountered exception to the rule that numbers over beams contract note-values is the following notation of the first measure in the above example:

Any larger irregular groups may be notated according to the previously stated principle: a number, or a number and bracket, contracts the notes to fill the available space.

Foreign patterns are named according to the numbers of notes they contain: *duplet, triplet, quadruplet, quintuplet, sextuplet, septuplet,* etc.

Sometimes the foreign pattern occupies the space of more than one beat. The patterns in such cases are called *broad triplets, broad quadruplets,* etc.

It can be seen from the diagram immediately preceding that the second note of a broad triplet comes just before the second beat. The exact distribution of foreign patterns occupying more than one beat can be shown if we diagram them against the number of units which is the product of the beats and tones involved. For example, in the above cases we have three tones against two beats. This distribution can be shown within six units (graph paper may be used for this purpose):

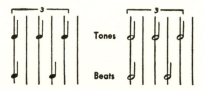

More involved cases may be solved in the same way. Here is four against three:

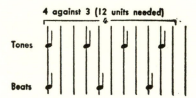

Beyond this point (five against four, six against five, etc.) the number of units needed is so great that the solutions, while possible on paper, are not apt to work out strictly in performance. Simultaneous arrival at the first point at which the tones and beats coincide is the most that can be expected.

EXPERIMENT 31.

Learn to perform three against two, and four against three. There are two methods:

a. Read the units of the graphs as though they were beats. Count six or twelve aloud, and tap the rhythms with your hands—the upper rhythm with the right hand, and the lower rhythm with the left hand. Begin very slowly on the first attempts, and gradually increase the speed until you are able to perform the rhythms as fast as you can count the units.

b. It may be noticed in performing the above rhythms that a composite pattern is formed, which includes the tapping of both hands. Following the composite patterns in learning to perform these rhythms may be even more helpful than counting the single units.

Three against two, with its six units shown as eighth-notes in $\frac{3}{4}$ meter, produces the composite pattern found below. In this illustration, upward stems indicate the right hand, downward stems the left hand, and double stems the two hands together.

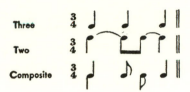

Four against three with its twelve units as eighth-notes in $\frac{12}{8}$ meter produces the following composite pattern:

CHAPTER

※ 7 ※

Syncopation

In Chapter 2 we saw that certain patterns in which the first tone did not coincide with the beat were called "syncopated." And in Chapter 5, on page 56, it was implied that syncopation occurred in an example which was shifted by two quarters away from its original position in relation to the metric accent. Neither of these references, nor the explanation of the origin of the term "syncopation" from the Greek *synkopē* ("a cutting up"), has given us a very definite idea as to the actual nature of syncopation. We have only the vague impression (which is correct enough) that it involves some kind of conflict between the notes and the beats. Since syncopation is one of the most difficult aspects of rhythmic performance, we shall try in this chapter to pin it down by close analysis, and by classification and grading of the various types in the order of difficulty.

DEFINITION

Syncopation results when the tones fail with some consistency to fall on the beats or on the points of metric accents. It is necessary to say "with some consistency" because the element of conflict results from the tendency of the syncopated notes to form a new order of beats or accents, overthrowing the one already present, and this tendency cannot arise except after more than one or two syncopated notes have occurred. For example, if one tone falls an eighth-rest after the beat, the existing meter will not be disturbed.

74

If two tones fall an eighth-rest behind the beat, some conflict arises.

If this goes on for a few measures, the urge of the tones to form a new order of beats coinciding with their positions in time is considerable, and the original beats hold their positions against the tones only with effort. In such cases, a genuine state of syncopated conflict exists.

It is easy to see why syncopated rhythms are hard to perform, since they challenge the power of the regulating beats. Even good musicians reading chamber music without a conductor can be thrown off by complicated syncopations which upset the meter, and make the counting of the beats unexpectedly difficult. On the other hand, jazz musicians, extemporaneously, and without the complications of notation, use every variety of "off-beat" playing. They find much pleasure in the conflict between the beat, which is kept steadily by the accompaniment, and the melody, which sometimes anticipates and sometimes delays, but seldom coincides exactly with the beat. The amount of syncopation which is usual in jazz performance would be, if notated exactly, extremely complicated to read—perhaps exceeding the most difficult examples which are to follow here.

CLASSIFICATION

As in other parts of this book, we shall try to overcome the difficulties of a complex problem by grading and classification, so that the problem may be solved in separate and shorter stages. To classify a syncopation we need to know two things about it:

1. We need to know the lengths of the tones in the syncopation. These lengths can be defined with our already established termi-

nology which relates all rhythmic quantities to the beat. The syncopated tones might be the length of the beat itself, the length of the
first multiplication, the length of the first division, the length of
the second division, etc. This factor (the length of the syncopated
tones) we shall call the *level* of the syncopation. For instance, in
the syncopated example given above (page 75), the syncopated
tones were quarter-notes, and the metric unit was a quarter-note.
Since the values of the syncopated tones and the beat are the same,
we say that the syncopation is on the level of the beat.

2. We need to know the amount of the time lag between the
beats and the syncopated tones. We shall call this factor the *displacement*, and define it by a fraction which shows its relation to
the level (i.e., to the lengths of the syncopated notes). For instance,
in the syncopated example given above (page 75), the level was
that of the beat (a quarter-note), and the time lag, or displacement,
was established by the eighth-rest at the beginning of the syncopation. Since this eighth-rest was one half the length of the syncopated
tones (quarter-notes), we indicate the displacement by the fraction
½.

This terminology is not labeling merely for the sake of labeling:
it gives us a means of estimating the difficulties of syncopations. If
we write music, we need to know the extent of the difficulties we
are creating for performers. If we perform, we must know how to
analyze these difficulties in order to overcome them.

EXAMPLES USING DUPLE VALUES

There are syncopations in which the note-values on the various
levels are all duple. Their intrinsic difficulty depends on two factors:

1. *The relation of the level to the beat.* If the level is the same or
larger than the beat, the syncopation will be easier. If the level is
that of any smaller part of the beat (first division, second division,
etc.), the syncopation will be more difficult.

2. *The size of the displacement.* The smaller the fraction of displacement, the more difficult the syncopation.

The examples below are arranged as closely as possible in the order of difficulty, and they are to be worked through according to the procedures outlined in Experiment 32, which immediately follows them.

1. Level: first multiplication
   Displacement: ½

2. Level: the beat
   Displacement: ½

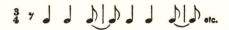

3. Level: first division
   Displacement: ½

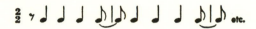

4. Level: first multiplication
   Displacement: ¼

5. Level: the beat
   Displacement: ¼

6. Level: second division
   Displacement: ½

7. Level: first multiplication
Displacement: ⅛

8. Level: first division
Displacement: ¼

Syncopation may take place within a foreign pattern. In such cases the displacement is usually the value of the first note of the pattern.

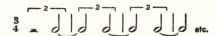

EXPERIMENT 32.

a. Write in the beats under each example, as follows:

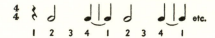

b. Perform each of the examples, increasing their lengths as much as necessary:
   (1) Clap the beats and sing the rhythms.
   (2) Say the beats and clap the rhythms.

c. Write examples of each kind of syncopation, using various meters, and practice performing them.

d. Take down the various syncopations by dictation. The procedure for this should be:

   (1) The performer announces the time signature, and performs the syncopation, tapping with two different objects, or singing and tapping the beats.

   (2) The listeners first determine the level. A valuable hint for this process is to remember that:

(a) If there are two beats per note of the syncopation, the
level is that of the first multiplication.

(b) If there is one beat between each note, the level is that
of the beat.

(c) If there are two notes between each beat, the level is
that of the first division.

(d) If there are four notes between each beat, the level is
that of the second division.

(3) The listeners determine the fraction of displacement. There
is no such valuable hint for this process. One must learn to
recognize the more usual displacement of $\frac{1}{2}$, and then try to
grasp the difficult short displacements by comparing them
with the more usual one.

(4) The notation follows after the determination of the level
and the displacement. This process should be relatively easy
if parts *b* and *c* of this experiment have been practiced sufficiently.

EXAMPLES USING TRIPLE VALUES

There are three kinds of triple groupings within which syncopations may occur: groups of three beats (bars of three beats, or
sections of bars of six, nine, or twelve in slow tempo), triple units
(dotted notes) which break down into three first-division notes,
and triplets which occur as foreign patterns where duple metric
units are used. In actual sound we can hear syncopations involving
triple groupings on only two levels: the triple measure (or section of
a measure), or the beat which breaks down into three parts, whether
it is a dotted note breaking down into three first-division notes, or
an undotted note breaking down into a triplet. Displacements in
these syncopations may be by $\frac{2}{3}$, $\frac{1}{3}$, or rarely $\frac{1}{6}$ of the lengths of
the tones.

The following examples are also arranged as closely as possible
in the order of difficulty. Again, this depends on the level (notes
which have the lengths of bars or sections of bars will be easier than
those lasting only one beat), and on the displacement (the shorter
the displacement, the more difficult the syncopation). The examples
are to be worked through as outlined in Experiment 33, which immediately follows them.

1. A triple bar displaced by ⅔ of its value.

2. A triple bar displaced by ⅓ of its value.

3. A triple unit displaced by ⅔ of its value.

4. A triplet displaced by ⅔ of its value.

5. A triple unit displaced by ⅓ of its value.

6. A triplet displaced by ⅓ of its value.

7. A triple bar displaced by ⅙ of its value.

8. A triple unit displaced by ⅙ of its value.

Examples 5 and 8 ($\frac{9}{4}$ and $\frac{12}{8}$) may also be performed in slow tempo, counting nine and twelve beats to the bar. In this case they would be much easier than their present listing implies.

EXPERIMENT 33.

a. Write in the beats under each of the above examples.

b. Perform each of the examples, increasing their lengths as much as necessary:

(1) Clap the beats and sing the rhythms.
(2) Say the beats and clap the rhythms.

c. Compose similar examples in different meters.

d. Take down these syncopations by dictation, using a procedure similar to the one in Experiment 32*d*, page 78.

All syncopations can be shown in notation (1) by the use of ties, (2) by notes including the full value of those tied together, or (3) by the use of rests. The pattern is not changed in sound except by the use of rests, which changes the articulation.

The syncopations shown thus far have all begun with rests, which makes the conception of displacement clearer. But the situation is the same if the rests are replaced by notes.

While all the examples given start at the beginnings of bars, there is nothing to prevent a syncopation from starting at any other point. For instance:

Very long beams are sometimes used in syncopations, although shorter beams linked together by ties reveal the structure of the measure more clearly.

Syncopations, of course, do not always occur in long sequences such as we have practiced here. Short syncopated groups of various types may be mixed in with all other kinds of rhythms. Mixtures of different types of syncopations with foreign patterns produce rhythms which sound as free from the influence of meter as if it did not exist. Try the following example, in slow tempo:

In the chapter which follows we shall learn to make larger rhythmic groups, such as the one above, in a graded sequence of difficulty, and thereby begin to apply all the separate rhythmical skills we have acquired in the past chapters to situations more closely resembling actual music.

If we were to draw an analogy between our rhythmical studies up to this point and a comparable study of language, we might say that so far we have learned to produce the vowel and consonant sounds of the language, to pronounce and understand a vocabulary of basic words, and to write these words according to the conventions of the language. Although we would have practiced long repetitive sequences of these words, we would not yet have put together anything corresponding to a meaningful sentence, paragraph, or any other larger structure. In this chapter we must extend our experience beyond the level of isolated "words" (rhythmic patterns, single measures of rhythms) to the level of more or less complete statements of rhythmical ideas. Our first problem in making this extension involves terminology.

THE PROBLEM OF FORM TERMINOLOGY

Music exists in the dimension of time, and all aspects of its temporal structure are referred to collectively as its *form*. The ingredients of the form are units of time which range in size from the length of the whole piece downward to the duration of the shortest note-value contained in the piece. While we have commonly agreed upon names for the smallest units (note-values, bars), and in a general way for the larger ones (sections, movements), there is no generally accepted terminology for the many other kinds of time units between the smallest and largest. To go back to the analogy with language, we have names for syllables and words, and for chapters and parts, but no specific and generally accepted terms corresponding to clause, sentence, or paragraph.

Mere names for these units have not been lacking; the terms

motive, phrase, and *period* have been used to some extent in this connection. But the difficulty has come with the application of these terms to music.

While music which is written down appears to be in a captive state in which it can be broken apart, analyzed, and labeled, its real essence has not actually been captured by notation. It can be deceptively easy to observe the divisions between sections of the musical structure on paper, but the *meanings* of these sections depend upon their existence in time, or, that is, upon actual sounding performance. A section which looks long enough on paper to qualify as a "paragraph" may in actual performance go by so quickly that it scarcely gives the impression of a "clause." Or a short-looking section may move so slowly as to create the impression of a substantial and complete statement. Therefore, counting the number of bars within formal units which are discernible on the written page will not tell us how to classify them. We cannot deal with problems of musical structure without taking into account their normal dimension, which is time.

The first necessity for theoretical analysis is a means of measurement. If, in dealing with musical structure, time is the quantity to be measured, we think immediately of a clock. But, unfortunately, the kind of time we deal with in music is not that of the clock but that of the mind; it is a kind of "psychological time" for which there is no mechanical means of measurement. In this kind of time terms such as "long" and "short" cannot be defined in minutes, because what is long or short is only what *seems* to be so. To make the situation still more complex, these impressions will vary not only according to the quality of the events being perceived during the time, but also according to the differing receptive abilities of the hearers.

Faced with so many variable elements, and lacking any objective means of measurement, music theory has been justifiably impotent in dealing with the question of musical form. Composers have used subjective means of measurement, or "instinct," and have not been particularly inconvenienced by the lack of theoretical basis for their work. But in the early stages of instruction, the lack of valid formulas is somewhat inconvenient. We face this situation now in beginning, without formulas, to construct formal units of sizes roughly corresponding to sentences or paragraphs. As form is basically a temporal matter, these phrases or periods, as they are often called, are expressed only in rhythmic outline, to be tapped or sung on one note. Later in this study, and in the study of harmony, it will be seen that the elements of melody and harmony do much to heighten and clarify the perception of musical form. In fact, since these non-temporal elements affect the passage of psychological time, they can themselves become form-building factors.

THE PHRASING SLUR

To aid us in the musical problem corresponding to the punctuation of sentences, there is a device called the *phrasing slur*. It is a curved line which is carried along next to the note-heads to show the lengths of phrases, or the subdivisions within phrases.

A combination of two curved lines, one placed over the other, may result if the phrase already contains a tie.

The latter may also be written as follows:

No exact rule can be given for the placement of phrasing slurs, since there may be disagreements as to the points at which rhythmic groups begin and end, and also as to whether the smallest or largest possible groupings should be emphasized in performance. Some players prefer the longest lines; others look for every possible subdivision. Disagreement of this kind is not undesirable, however, since it contributes to variety in performance.

There are, in spite of the ambiguities of any given situation, three possible guides to normal phrasing:

1. *Rests or long tones*. Either of these factors will produce natural pauses which will make the rhythmic structure less ambiguous.

2. *Breathing*. The limits of the breath may aid us in determining the placement of phrasing slurs when rests and long tones are missing.

3. *Repetitions*. Repetitions guide the attention, and make easier the delineation of the rhythmic groups.

Experiment 34.

Mark the phrasing of the following rhythmic examples, using phrasing slurs:

a. The rest in this example shows a main division. Sing the example at a moderate speed, and locate the other smaller subdivisions within the two main parts.

b. Sing this undefined stream of eighth-notes rather slowly, and try to find the most logical place to take a breath.

c. This is the rhythmic pattern of a familiar song ("America"). Observe how the repetition of a two-bar group at the beginning establishes a pattern of organization in two-bar groups which prevails throughout the piece.

There are special uses of slur lines which add to the confusion already surrounding the phrasing slur. The special uses of slurs in vocal music will be discussed in Chapters 10 and 13, while the uses of slurs for various orchestral instruments will be discussed in some detail in Appendix II. Here is a brief summary of the general instrumental uses, intended simply to give an idea of the variety of meanings conveyed by the slur line:

1. *Keyboard instruments.* Short slurs simply enclose notes that are to be played with a smooth, unbroken style of articulation. Long slurs may be indications of phrases.

2. *String instruments.* Slurs indicate specifically the number of notes to be played in one upward or downward stroke of the bow. They do *not* indicate phrasing, since a string player may connect separate bow strokes very smoothly, or, on the other hand, may employ various kinds of accented articulations within one single stroke.

3. *Wind instruments.* Long slurs may indicate the number of tones to be played smoothly on one breath. Short slurs, however, do not indicate breathing, but, rather, the articulation. On wind instruments a great variety of short groupings and detached tones may be played within single long breaths, using the tongue to stop momentarily the flow of air into the mouthpiece. These long breaths, during which the tone is stopped, are not usually indicated by slurs.

RHYTHMIC PHRASES: NOTATION, PROCEDURE

We shall try in Experiment 35 to compose phrases in rhythmic outline. Certain problems of notation may now occur which have not concerned us up to this point:

1. A note occupying a full measure is placed in the middle, or slightly to the left of the middle, of the bar. This rule applies to single-line music only. If other parts are involved, as in harmony, the note is placed where it actually occurs in relation to the other parts, i.e., at the beginning of the measure.

2. The rest for a full measure is the whole-rest for all time signatures smaller than $\frac{4}{2}$. For $\frac{4}{2}$, or rare larger meters such as $\frac{5}{2}$, the breve-rest is used.* These rests are, without exception, placed in the middle of the bar.

3. Phrases may begin on beats other than the first beat of the measure. The incomplete bar at the beginning is compensated by another incomplete bar at the end. The two incomplete bars add up to one whole-bar.

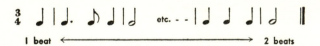

* The breve-rest when used for a meter smaller than $\frac{4}{2}$ means *two* bars' rest. For various practically obsolete signs indicating more than two bars' rest, see Appendix IV, page 274.

The preliminary notes are called "up-beats." If the first measure is so nearly complete that the compensating tone at the end would be too short (less than half of a duple measure, or less than two thirds of a triple measure), the first measure is filled out with rests, and the last measure is written out in full.

4. If a change of meter occurs at the end of a staff, it should be marked both after the end of the staff and at the beginning of the next staff.

Older editions use the sectional double-bar (‖) in front of each new meter. This practice is based on the assumption, no longer valid, that changes of meter are most apt to occur at dividing points in the form.

The rhythmic phrases which we are to compose will need indications of tempo and character fully as much as if they were real pieces, as it is intended that they be practiced in performance, not merely written on paper. Such indications are usually placed above the staff at the beginning of a piece. We may use words to describe the character of the phrase,* such as "Bright," "Slow," "Gay," "Sad," etc., together with a metronome mark to give the specific tempo.

* A glossary of Italian, French, and German terms indicating character, tempo, and "expression" will be found in Appendix IV, pages 259–269.

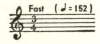

The letters M. M. sometimes found with the metronome mark in older editions mean "Maelzel Metronome," referring to the inventor of the mechanical metronome (see footnote, page 19).

The difficulty of the phrases may be regulated by controlling the following factors:

1. Meter (time signature).
2. The speed of the fastest notes (level of division).
3. The conflict between meter (beat) and rhythm (note-durations), as produced by syncopated and foreign patterns.

Begin with simple examples (easy, unchanging meters, notes at the speed of the beats or less, and no syncopations or foreign patterns), and progress to more difficult combinations, mastering the performance of each phrase as you compose it.

EXPERIMENT 35.

Compose phrases in rhythmic outline, taking into account the factors mentioned above. Use the phrasing slur as a guide for breathing, and to show the subdivisions within the phrases.

RHYTHMIC PRACTICE

The rhythmic phrases composed in Experiment 35 should be used for sight-reading and dictation. Students may exchange papers for sight-reading (this places a proper emphasis on clear and accurate notation as well as legible writing), and individual students may perform their phrases for the whole group for dictation.

For additional practice, and as illustrations of the kind of material to be produced in Experiment 35, rhythmic examples are given on the following pages. They are arranged in an order of increasing difficulty, and may therefore serve to test rhythmic facility. In working through them, each stage should be mastered before the next is attempted, and each group of examples may be extended as much as necessary by composing new phrases according to the procedures of Experiment 35.

The student who is able to perform all of these examples after a little practice has mastered a large part of his course of rhythmic training. With additional practice at the mere process of keeping his eye properly trained on the page, he will surely develop into a good reader. On the other hand, the student who is able to perform only the simpler examples, and finds himself blocked at a certain point, will at least know what that point is, and will at least be able to see what obstacles lie ahead of him in rhythmic training. The method given here of isolating and grading rhythmic difficulties offers him a way to set progressively more difficult tasks for himself, and he can take as long as he needs to arrive at the desired final goal.

The methods of performance for these examples should be as follows:

1. Sing "la" or "ta" and clap the beats.
2. Clap the rhythms and count aloud.
3. Count the beats and play at the keyboard (on one tone).

Phrasing slurs are used in these examples mainly as guides for breathing when they are sung.

I. No syncopations, and no divisions except the first division in compound meters.

II. Second divisions, and more dotted notes, but no syncopations. Regular meters.

Gay (♩ = 108)

Vigorous (♩ = 88)

III. Syncopations at the levels of the first multiplication and the beat. No very short displacements.

Moderate (♩ = 116)

Brisk (♪ = 108)

Fast (♩ = 144)

Slow (♩. = 66)

IV. Syncopations at the level of the first and second divisions, and with shorter displacements. Third divisions.

* A dotted line is used in these exercises for two-note slurs which might be mistaken for ties.

V. Foreign patterns, and irregular and changing meters. More conflict between meter and rhythm.

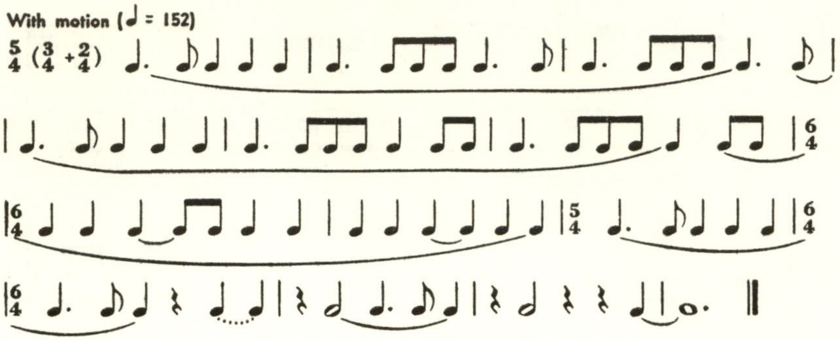
With motion (♩ = 152)

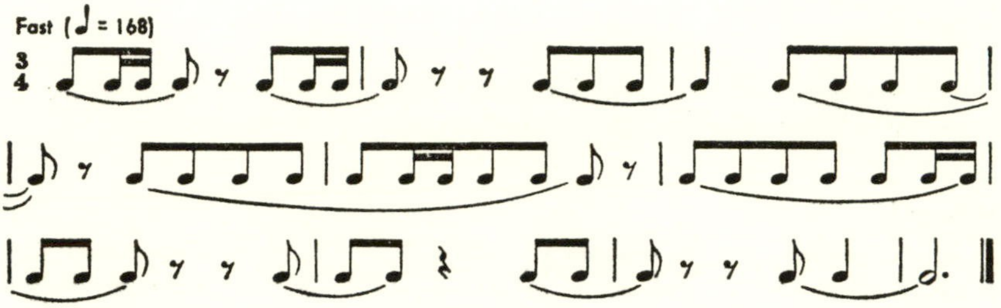
Fast (♩ = 168)

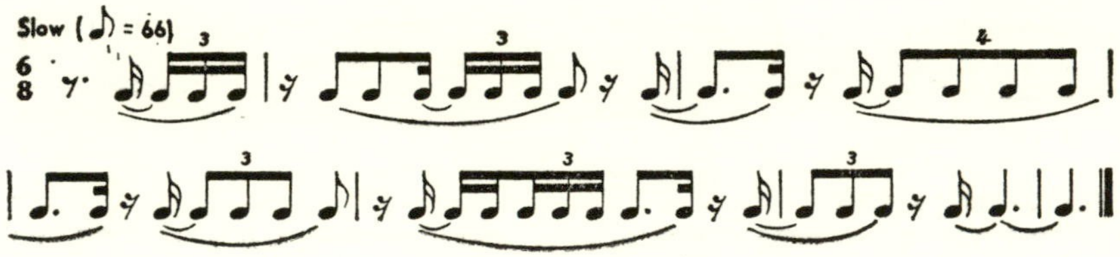
Slow (♪ = 66)

PART TWO

Scales and Melody
PROJECTS IN MELODY WRITING

CHAPTER

❧9❧

Scales in General: Melodic Successions

One might assume from our approach to musical material thus far that larger and larger units may be derived from smaller units, and that the process would be one of simple addition. This assumption is incorrect, however; because if the additive process is used with musical material, the results always total something more than simple addition would imply, and the individual units themselves are modified in the process. Musical materials can best be compared to fluids which flow together and react upon each other.

With musical materials, of course, this merging takes place in the mind. Each new impression joins earlier impressions. Each new impression is judged in terms of the old ones, and the old ones are reevaluated in terms of the new. No single musical experience can remain really isolated from the others which surround it.

SCALE DERIVATION

If we examine any melodic succession of three or more tones (keeping in mind the fluid nature of the medium), we find that besides the intervals which occur in direct succession others are formed between nonadjacent tones. At the end of the succession a higher unit will also have been created which is the sum of all the tones and intervals involved. For example, the illustration below contains in direct succession a major third and a minor third. A fifth occurs *indirectly* between the first and last tones, and the whole progression adds up to the higher unit shown in black notes.

99

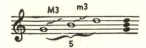

Here are the tones (without rhythm) of a folk-melody * which begins with the same three notes. It proceeds through its whole course with the addition of only one other new tone (E).

A tonal extract consisting of all the tones in this melody would be as follows:

The formalized representation of a tonal extract of this kind is known as a *scale* (Latin: *scala*, ladder). To put the above extract in scale form, we would need to (1) determine the most conspicuous and important tone in the group; (2) arrange the tones in ascending order through one octave, beginning with the most important tone.

The determination of the most important tone is a very complex process if carried out on a strictly theoretical basis. We can, for the present, do it more or less by "ear" and by observing two factors which usually tend to emphasize tones. One of these factors is repetition. A tone heard more often than the others may impress itself more firmly upon the memory. The other factor is prominent position. A tone occurring at the beginning, at the end of a section, and especially at the end of the whole piece, will get more attention and achieve correspondingly more prominence than its neighbors.

If we observe these factors in the preceding folk-melody we must conclude that G is the most prominent tone, although it is challenged somewhat by E.

The formalized scale for this melody would be:

* See complete form on page 111.

The question logically arises now as to which is first in the natural order—a scale or a melody. In the case of the above tune or almost any other folk-tune originated and preserved simply by singing, the melody must have come into existence without consciousness of an underlying scale. And yet it is obvious that folk-singers are held within some sorts of tonal limits, whether they are conscious of these limits or not. What, for example, could have held the singer of the song quoted above within the narrow path he followed?

An examination of the interval content of the melody shows us that the singer avoided all the most complicated intervals. There are no major sevenths, minor seconds, or tritones, either directly or indirectly. This is undoubtedly our clue: the singer relied on his feeling for simple interval relationships, and followed what was the line of least resistance for him at his particular level of musical development.

TONAL ORDERS

The process followed by this folk-singer in forming his melody is essentially the same one followed by all musicians on all levels, not only in our own culture but in others as well. Intervals are the raw material of sound given to us by nature, and the process of tonal evolution is simply the gradual understanding and utilization of the various intervals and their possible combinations in melody and harmony. Research in the music of various cultures (called ethnomusicology), historical research, and theoretical investigation within the sphere of Western music alone seem to show that this evolution progresses through well-defined stages. Within each stage a whole orderly system of music may exist before human impatience forces its way over the threshold into the next stage, in which the new system absorbs the old one and forms its own new laws.

We have already encountered these stages in a rudimentary way as the three tonal orders—pentatonic, diatonic, and chromatic—which are expressed visibly in the arrangement of the keys on the piano. Our discussion at that point relied mainly on the fact that the number of tones increases within the orders from five to seven to twelve. These numbers implied a progression from simple to complex without really explaining why such was the case. Actually the number of tones involved has little to do with the level of tonal complexity. The pentatonic order, for example, is simple not because it contains only five tones, but rather because these certain five tones make among themselves only relatively simple intervals. The use of one or the other of the tonal orders by musicians of a given period or culture will result, then, from the feeling these musicians have (or do not have) for the intervals and their combinations, and the tonal orders can really be defined only in terms of their interval contents.

The character of a tonal order is determined as much by the intervals it excludes as by those it includes. Here are descriptions of the three orders on that basis:

1. *Pentatonic.* The scale of a melody conforming to this order consists of five different tones. It contains three whole-steps and two leaps of minor thirds. It does not contain half-steps, major sevenths, or tritones.

2. *Diatonic.* Scales belonging to this order contain seven different tones in regular stepwise order (i.e., no gaps of a minor third, as in the pentatonic scales). There are five whole-steps and two half-steps within an octave, with the half-steps kept some distance from each other. Not more than one half-step is found within any group of four tones. Each diatonic scale also contains one tritone.*

3. *Chromatic.* This tonal order may be best defined at this point in almost entirely negative terms. We must escape the idea at once that the chromatic order can be simply and positively defined as a mere sequence of twelve tones arranged in half-step succession (the chromatic scale). Much smaller combinations of tones than this may exceed the limits of diatonicism as they are defined above, and thereby express the chromatic order. For example, combinations of three or four tones may produce nondiatonic groupings such as two

* In two cases—the scales from B to b and F to f—the scales contain both forms of the diatonic tritone (diminished fifth and augmented fourth). Partly for this reason, the scale B to b is rarely used.

half-steps within the space of a fourth, or two different tritones within an octave. At a later stage we shall discuss other typical chromatic groupings, arriving finally at a positive and more complete definition. Until then we may rely on a primitive but accurate distinction between diatonic and chromatic which once again makes use of the keyboard: since the white keys of the piano are arranged according to the diatonic order, *any group of tones which cannot at some point be played on the white keys alone must be chromatic.*

EXPERIMENT 36.

Try to find these three-note combinations on the keyboard. Discover which one cannot be played without the use of a black key, and is, therefore, chromatic. The tones are numbered 1, 2, 3 from the lowest to the highest. The intervals between 1 and 2, and 2 and 3, are singled out by brackets.

$$
\begin{array}{llll}
3 \left\{ \begin{array}{l} m\,3 \\[4pt] \end{array} \right. & 3 \left\{ \begin{array}{l} 5 \\[4pt] \end{array} \right. & 3 \left\{ \begin{array}{l} M\,3 \\[4pt] \end{array} \right. & 3 \left\{ \begin{array}{l} m\,3 \\[4pt] \end{array} \right. \\
2 \left\{ \begin{array}{l} M\,3 \end{array} \right. & 2 \left\{ \begin{array}{l} m\,3 \end{array} \right. & 2 \left\{ \begin{array}{l} M\,3 \end{array} \right. & 2 \left\{ \begin{array}{l} 4 \end{array} \right. \\
1 & 1 & 1 & 1
\end{array}
$$

SCALE POSSIBILITIES

Since a tonal order is a more general category than a scale, numerous scales can be formed within each order. In fact, a different one can be formed on each tone of an order, which means that there can be five pentatonic scales, seven diatonic scales, and twelve chromatic scales. Each of these scales would have a different arrangement of steps, except the chromatic, in which, according to our present tonal system, there could be only twelve equal half-steps, regardless of the starting point.*

* This discrepancy has not failed to attract the attention of speculative theorists. Joseph Yasser, in a book called *A Theory of Evolving Tonality* (American Library of Musicology, 1932), proposed filling the octave with nineteen tones which would be slightly more than a quarter of a tone apart. Out of these nineteen tones, a dozen twelve-note scales could be derived which would be distinguished by different patterns of small intervals. Each scale would contain, in various arrangements, seven half-steps of approximately the size we know and five smaller steps of approximately a quarter-tone.

The scales of the various kinds of folk-music as well as the scale systems of cultivated art music, then, are nothing more than selections from the total number of abstract possibilities. We shall deal more specifically with some of the scale systems of well-known usage in the chapters to follow, but, as a general introduction to the scale types, let us work out the abstract possibilities in the following experiment:

EXPERIMENT 37.

a. As we have seen before, the arrangement of the tones in the gamut (all white keys) is diatonic. If we omit two of these tones within an octave (and they are the right two tones) we can produce pentatonic scales on the white keys. These scales will sound like the others so easily produced by brushing the hand across the black keys.

According to the list of exclusions for the pentatonic order, write, play, and sing ascending pentatonic scales through one octave beginning on A, B, C, D, E, F, and G.

b. We can make diatonic scales from the tones of the gamut, beginning on any white key and proceeding upward through one octave.

Write, play, and sing diatonic scales beginning on A, B, C, D, E, F, and G.

Diagram the step patterns and indicate the tritone in each scale according to this model:

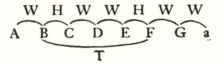

c. Although we have no means of notating chromatic groupings at this point, certain patterns may be produced by playing all seven of the diatonic tones plus one or more of the intervening black keys. Try playing and singing some of these scales, and observe their curious effects.

MELODIC SUCCESSIONS: NOTATION, PROCEDURE

Just as composing and performing rhythmic phrases in Chapter 8 extended our previous skills within the rhythmic sphere, composing and performing melodic successions made from the various kinds of scales will extend our previous skills within the tonal sphere. The following experiments and exercises in this way parallel those given at the end of Chapter 8. To achieve similar results through progressively arranged problems, we must find a method of classifying melodic difficulties which parallels the classification of rhythmic problems employed in Chapter 8.

A melody, in its most basic definition, is simply a chain of intervals strung out horizontally. The tones, as we have seen before, may be added up to produce the higher organizational units which we call scales. The scales, in turn, belong to one or another of the still higher organizational units which we call tonal orders. Therefore, the difficulty of a melodic line as far as singing is concerned (omitting all rhythmic factors) must be determined on these three planes: its difficulty must be judged according to its use of intervals (especially the melodic leaps), and according to the complexity of both its scale and tonal order.

In the experiment which is to follow, we shall compose melodic successions within the pentatonic and diatonic scales of Experiment 37. We may control the difficulty of the melodic leaps by the following set of regulations, which establish certain thresholds for melodic motion. In the various stages of the graded melodic successions, allow:

1. No leaps larger than thirds.
2. No leaps larger than a fifth (no tritone leaps in the diatonic melodies).
3. No leaps of sevenths, the tritone, or intervals larger than an octave.
4. No leaps larger than a twelfth (all smaller leaps permitted).

Besides the regulation of leaps, two other tonal considerations may be included:

1. Maintain a sense of variety in the melodies by avoiding too many repetitions of the same tones.
2. Give the melodies a rudimentary sense of organization by beginning and ending on the same tone.

For the notation of these melodic successions, use only whole-notes, without time signatures or bar-lines, and make use of each of the four principal clefs.

The number of melodies to be composed, as well as the emphasis on one kind or another, can be decided according to the needs of individuals or groups.

EXPERIMENT 38.

Compose pentatonic and diatonic melodic successions of eight to sixteen notes, based on the scales of Experiment 37, and graded in the manner suggested above.

MELODIC PRACTICE

The melodic successions composed in the above experiment should be used for singing, playing (at the piano), and dictation practice.

The following procedure may be used for dictation:

1. The name of the first tone and the clef are announced.

2. The melody is played through in slow tempo (six or eight beats per tone) as many times as necessary, depending on the difficulty of the melody and the ability of the class. If played on the piano, the connections between the tones are better understood when each tone is repeated immediately before it moves ahead to the next tone.

3. The listeners take down the notes on staff paper, or in a short-hand which shows the direction of melody and intervals involved. Here is a melody shown in staff and shorthand notation:

Steps are shown as W and H, rather than as M2 and m2.

For additional practice, here are some examples of melodic successions arranged in the order of difficulty given for Experiment 38. Since these examples are written in various clefs, they will not be suited in singing practice to all voice ranges. Therefore, when they are used in that way, men may sing the treble and alto clefs an octave lower, and women may sing the bass and tenor clefs an octave higher. If there are instances in which even this procedure fails to bring the melodies into the ranges of the singers, they may be sung beginning on any comfortable pitches, simply maintaining the correct interval relationships between the tones. For keyboard practice and dictation, the exercises should be played and taken down as written.

I   Pentatonic Melodic Successions

A. No leaps larger than thirds.

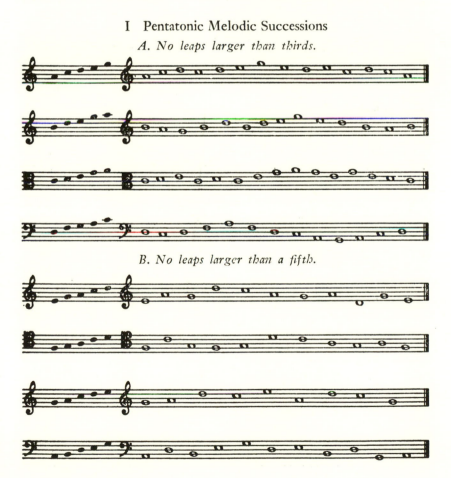

B. No leaps larger than a fifth.

C. *No leaps larger than sixths, except the octave.*

D. *All leaps up to a twelfth.*

II Diatonic Melodic Successions

A. *No leaps larger than a third.*

B. No leaps larger than a fifth; no tritone leaps.

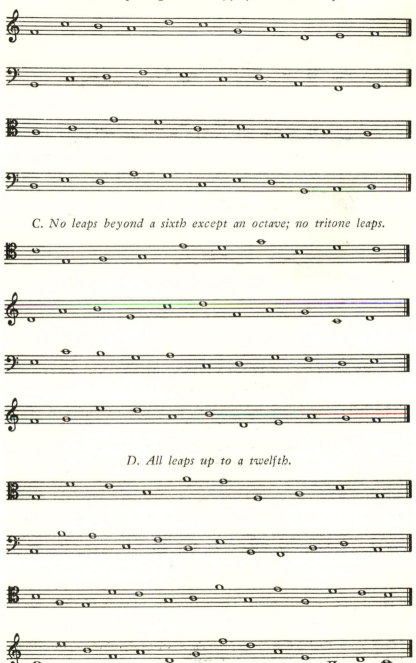

C. No leaps beyond a sixth except an octave; no tritone leaps.

D. All leaps up to a twelfth.

III   Chromatic Melodic Successions (in shorthand notation)

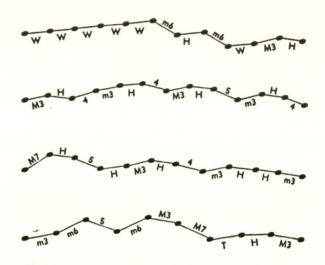

EXAMPLES OF PENTATONIC, DIATONIC AND CHROMATIC MELODIES

The following folk-songs provide authentic examples of pentatonic and diatonic melodies. All of these pieces were collected by the great English folk-song collector, Cecil Sharp,* in mountain areas of the southeast United States which had been practically isolated since they were settled some two hundred years earlier. Some of the melodies and texts are of very ancient origin, having been brought over from England and Scotland by the early settlers. According to Sharp, they survived better in these isolated areas than in modern industrialized England. We can be grateful that Sharp preserved these melodies when he did (1916–17), because very likely the areas through which he traveled have since been invaded by phonographs and radios. These devices, in spite of their advantages, do remove the incentive to sing, which is the life source of

* Cecil Sharp, *English Folk Songs from the Southern Appalachians,* two volumes (New York: Oxford University Press, 1932).

folk-melody. Probably most of these songs are already lost to the sons and daughters of the mountaineers who sang them for Sharp.

Experiment 39.

Sing these melodies, and derive the scales for Numbers 2 to 6 in the same manner that the scale for Number 1 ("I'm Going to Georgia") was derived at the beginning of this chapter.

1. "I'm Going to Georgia" (No. 78 B, sung by Miss Lillian Ogle, Berea, Madison Co., Ky., May 23, 1917).

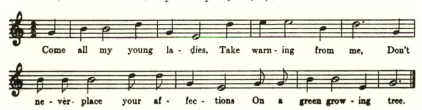

2. "The Lonesome Prairie" (No. 169 A, sung by Mrs. Polly Patrick at Hart's Creek, Manchester, Clay Co., Ky., August 14, 1917).

3. "Locks and Bolts" (No. 80 C, sung by Miss Linny Landers at Carmen, N. C., Sept. 5, 1916).

4. "George Reilly" (No. 82 A, sung by Mrs. Jane Gentry, Hot Springs, N. C., August 24, 1916).

As I walked out one sum-mer's morn-ing To view and take the pleas-ant air, I___ saw a girl, and a come-ly___ fair one: She ap-peared to me some li - ly fair.

5. "Whistle, Daughter, Whistle" (No. 134, sung by Mrs. Margaret Jack Dodd, Beachgrove, Virginia, May 25, 1918).

1. Whis - tle, whis - tle, daugh - ter, and you shall have a sheep. I can - not whis - tle, mo - ther, nor nei - ther will I yet. Whis - tle, whis - tle, daugh - ter, and you shall have a cow I can - not whis - tle, mo - ther, nor nei - ther will I now.

Verse 2 *

Whistle, whistle, daughter, and you shall have a man.
(*Whistles*)
O you saucy jade, what makes you whistle now?
O mother, I'd rather have a man than have a sheep or cow.

* This is the complete text for this song, given in full because it is short. All the other songs quoted here have more verses, which may be seen in Sharp's collection.

6. "The Keys of Heaven" (No. 92 B, sung by Hester House, Hot Springs, N. C., September 16, 1916).

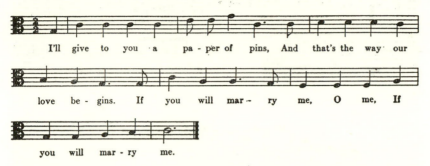

The following chromatic melodies are from the Fourth String Quartet * by Arnold Schoenberg (1874–1950), who was the leader of the chromatic composers during the first half of the the twentieth century. These melodies are given here simply to complete the representation of the various scale types, and for future reference, although they involve problems of notation which are beyond us at this point. By trying to sing them from the shorthand notation, however, we can gain some idea of the complexity of the chromatic idiom. It should go without saying, of course, that there are many gradations (even in the works of Schoenberg) between the practically pure chromaticism shown here and pure diatonicism.

* Published by G. Schirmer, N. Y., 1939.

CHAPTER

☙ 10 ❧

Church Modes. Melody-Writing Modeled on Gregorian Chant

The first part of this text was concerned with basic definitions, problems of notation, and problems involving performance. For these matters there was little choice of approach: definitions and notation data had to be stated so that they could be learned; and for the performance problems, material for practice had to be provided. While there are many ways of stating the necessary facts, and there are many kinds of material which can be provided for practice, this approach is essentially the only one for these aspects of music study.

Now, however, we are about to begin another aspect for which there are two distinct and different approaches. We shall in this chapter attempt to write melodies which will be more than the abstract chains of intervals used for singing and dictation practice in the preceding chapter. We shall, although on a small scale, come face to face at this point with actual creative problems. Before we do so it may be helpful to discuss the two approaches which music theory offers to these problems. We shall thereby gain a better perspective on the methods and procedures employed here, as well as on those which we may encounter later in more advanced studies.

PRELIMINARY: TWO APPROACHES TO COMPOSITION TECHNIQUE

One of the two approaches to composition technique examines musical material on its own terms, trying to discover the inherent nature of tonal combinations, and seeking to reveal the whole range of possibilities. This approach contains no "dos" or "don'ts"; it simply describes the material and the results to be expected from various procedures, and leaves all choices to the aesthetic judgment of the composer. This approach is detached from any particular practice of the past or present, and in a sense is a dry affair. However, for the student with a creative flair, it can ultimately be the most satisfactory kind, as it provides the maximum technical help while allowing the maximum freedom of aesthetic choice. To draw an analogy with architecture, this sort of theory would supply the necessary information about building materials (wood, stone, steel), all the necessary engineering knowledge about handling the materials, and the general principles of design. But it would not tell the architect how to make a Gothic building, a Colonial building, or one in any other particular style. Style would result from the architect's aesthetic choices; and he would have made these choices more or less unconsciously in response to the nature of his materials and his cultural background and environment. We might call this the "abstract" approach to theory, without, however, intending to imply that the results achieved by using it are necessarily abstract.

The second approach utilizes the ingredient least considered in the first approach—that is, style. This approach begins by dissecting a work of art in an effort to discover the principles underlying its construction. There is a certain comforting warmth in this kind of study, as a steady contact is maintained with living music. On the other hand, because the main concern in this approach is manner, not substance it may be difficult to separate the temporary, modish elements characteristic only of the taste of the time in which the work was created from the essential and universal principles on which rests the solid and permanent validity of the work. In order to reproduce a particular style, one must be told to do this and not to do that, not because there is anything essentially right or wrong about a given procedure, but simply because it was done that way in the particular stylistic model one is following.

Actually, since both of these approaches have advantages and disadvantages, one may be appropriate at one stage of study and the other may be just what is needed at another stage. Also, some mixing of the two approaches almost inevitably takes place, to the benefit of both. Some reference to real music can help to color an abstract approach, while some reduction to essentials can help to clarify the myriad detailed procedures of a stylistic approach.

To return to our own specific problem, we had already gone a short way toward an abstract approach to scales and melody in the preceding chapter. Diatonic scales, for example, were derived by a sort of permutation of the diatonic tones which gave us a complete view of the possibilities. No particular connection was established with music, however, and no estimates were made as to the usefulness of the various forms of the scale. Likewise we wrote melodic lines with a purely schematic approach to interval leaps and scale forms, omitting both aesthetic and stylistic considerations. This approach served us well enough at the time, but it will now be advantageous to adopt the other one, which brings in the element of style, and which will place our abstract knowledge in contact with a living body of music. The first necessity for accomplishing this is to find a model on which we can base specific technical and stylistic procedures; and for this model we can do no better than turn to the largest organized melodic repertoire within our culture—the ancient liturgical chant of the Roman Catholic Church.

THE MODEL: GREGORIAN CHANT

Roman chant, also called *Gregorian chant* * in honor of Pope Gregory I (d. 604) who especially encouraged its collection into an organized repertoire, has a certain pleasing appropriateness for the early stages of theory study because most of the earliest forms of Western music grew up as elaborations or imitations of it. Gregorian chant is the fountain from which our whole musical culture springs, very much as Latin is the source for the Romance languages. But besides this pleasing appropriateness, there are solid practical reasons why Gregorian chant provides an excellent basis for beginning the study of melody. For one thing, there is a huge written-down collection of these pieces (over 2,500 of them) to which we can refer. For another thing, we can turn directly to certain theorists who have already laid down many of the essential facts we need to know for composition in that style.

The earliest treatises dealing with chant date from about 800 A.D.

* Still other names: *plainsong*, or *plainchant*, from the Latin *cantus planus*.

They are concerned mainly with two problems: the tonal system, and, later on, the notation. The solutions found for these problems in the medieval treatises were the foundation on which Western music grew, although the authors themselves (all of whom were monks) were not attempting to build such a foundation. Their concern was not for the future technical development of music, but simply for the standardization of the practice of liturgical chant, which in their time had developed a confusing number of regional varieties because of the absence of a specific notation, and because of poor communication between widely separated monasteries. Part of this process of standardization was the elimination of "corrupt" elements which had crept into many chant melodies. In order to point out what was corrupt, the early theorists had to define very clearly what was "normal," and in laying down the principles by which chant melodies were to be normalized and classified, they also gave just the kind of information needed for the construction of such melodies. We are fortunate, therefore, in being able to turn to these theorists for clear statements from which we can form rules and procedures for our own first attempts at stylistically regulated melody-writing.

The theorist on whom we shall draw most heavily here is Odo, Abbot of Cluny in France (927–42). His treatise called *Enchiridion musices* * ("Handbook on Music") had the distinction of introducing the use of Latin letter names for the tones, the method we still use today. It also gave one of the clearest early accounts of the tonal system of chant melody.

The tonal system of chant melody was made up of a number of scalelike formulas which accounted not only for the tones employed in the melody but also for ranges and points of tonal emphasis. They were, therefore, more than the equivalents of the scales we derived from the folk-tune examples in the preceding chapter, and we do not use the word "scale" to describe them. The word used for them correctly implies that they contain not only the tones of the melodies but also some of the elements of a melodic style; they are called *modes*. The full definition of all the characteristics of a mode evolved rather gradually through several centuries, but the most important ones were already fully described in Odo's early treatise.

* The *Enchiridion* is available in English translation by Oliver Strunk (*Source Readings in Music History*. New York: W. W. Norton & Co., Inc., 1950).

MODES

Odo of Cluny says, "*A . . . mode is a rule which classes every melody according to its final.*"

The "final," of course, is the ending tone. We see here an illustration of the tendency of the mind to organize tones in order of relative importance. The final tone is heard last, and gains importance over the others because it lingers in the memory. Therefore, it becomes the focal point by which the remaining tones are organized.

The next most conspicuous tone, the first one, is also acknowledged in Odo's definition. "*Beginnings, too,*" he says, "*are found most often and most suitably on the sound which concludes the melody.*"

An agreement between the two most conspicuous tones would be a very important means of establishing a definite tonal focus. But certain other conspicuous points in the melody must also concur in the decision if complete tonal organization is to be achieved. Chant melodies are usually long enough to consist of a number of sections, each of which has a conspicuous ending tone. To account for these endings Odo says, "*Several distinctions* [secondary endings] *ought to end with the sound which concludes the mode, the masters teach, for if more distinctions be made in some other sound than be made in this one, they desire the melody to be ended in that other sound and compel it to be changed from the mode in which it was. A melody, in other words, belongs most to the mode in which the majority of its distinctions lie.*"

From these statements we derive our first rule for modal melody.

> RULE 1. *Usually begin, and always end, on the final.*
> *Maintain a balance of phrase-endings in favor of*
> *this tone.*

Not every tone in the gamut is available as a final. Only four centrally located notes may serve this purpose, according to the early system of church modes; they are D, E, F, and G.

Each final serves as the central point of two modes, which are different in range. In one kind, called *authentic modes*, the range extends upward to the octave above, and includes one other tone a whole-step below the final. In the other kind, called *plagal modes*, the range extends upward a fifth (or sixth), and includes tones down to the fifth below the final.*

The second rule for modal melody is:

RULE 2. *A melody must lie within the range of its mode.*

If the final is the tone toward which a melody gravitates at the end when its energy is spent, there is another tone in each mode which serves the opposite purpose, and toward which the melody drives while it is in an active state of development. This other important tone is called the *dominant.* Its position in relation to the final varies from mode to mode. The rule for locating the dominants is:

1. *For authentic modes*—a fifth above the final.
2. *For plagal modes*—a third below the dominant of the corresponding authentic mode.
3. *The exception*—the tone b, if it occurs in either of the above calculations, is always replaced by c. (The stigma attached to b seems to have come from its association with the tritones F-b and b-f.)

The dominants did not reach this standardized form until after Odo of Cluny: he does not mention them. They do, however, lend the modes character and individuality which might otherwise be lacking. For instance, the authentic mode on D, and the plagal mode on G, which have the same range, are distinguished particularly by the difference in their dominants.

The third rule for modal melody is:

RULE 3. *In the course of a melody emphasize the dominant. Give the dominant preference in phrase-endings not occurring on the final itself.*

Here is a chart giving the ranges, finals, and dominants of the modes. They are arranged and numbered as Odo suggests: in pairs according to the finals.

---

* The tone GG (a fifth below the final D) is a regular part of the gamut as given by Odo. This tone, which was the lowest of the gamut, had the Greek letter Γ (gamma). The tones above this were named as given in Chapter 1, starting with A and continuing up to *aa*.

(Tones in parentheses are possible extensions of the plagal ranges.)

MELODIC MOTION

Chant melody generally prefers stepwise motion to leaping, and such leaps as do occur are limited in scope, and are employed only where vocal energy is at its height: i.e., during the course of a phrase.

Our fourth rule for chant melody, in conformity with the demands of the smoothest vocal style, is:

RULE 4. *Stepwise motion should predominate. No leaps larger than a fifth in the course of a melody. No ascending leaps to the final tone in endings; no descending leaps to the final tone in endings, except the minor third.*

While chant melodies use diatonic tonal material, a great many of them show a strong residue of pentatonic feeling. This is expressed in the avoidance of any emphasis on the tritone or half-step progressions, which are the very elements of diatonicism that distinguish it from pentatonicism.

Direct tritone leaps are completely avoided in chant melody. Discrimination against half-steps is not so drastic, being limited to the avoidance of the ending progression E-F in Modes V and VI. The most complex restriction has to do with the avoidance of tritones between nonadjacent tones of the melody.

Unless four or more tones separate the notes of the tritone, they may still be perceived together through accumulative listening.

Some of the most easily perceived tritones in a melodic line are the following:

1. A four-note scale passage outlining the tritone.

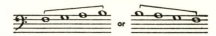

2. Or groups of three of these same tones.

3. The above groups combined with d or D.

ACCIDENTALS

Many chant melodies which lie in the area in which the avoidance of these melodic formulas would be too restrictive employ an alteration which lowers the tone b by a half-step. This lowered tone makes a perfect fourth with F instead of a tritone.

	Tritone				Perfect fourth	

Tritone   *Perfect fourth*

W W W   W W H

F   G   a   b   becomes   F   G   a   b

(high)   (low)

The symbol for lowering a tone by a half-step, called a *flat,*
descended from this period, when two forms of the letter b were
used to distinguish between the high and low positions of this tone.

    ♮ (square b) was the high, or *natural* form.

    ♭ (round b) was the low or *flatted* form.

We now show the two tones by placing somewhat similar signs
after an ordinary letter: b♮ is *b-natural,* and b♭ is *b-flat.** The natural
sign is not used unless it is needed to cancel a previous flat. The signs
are called *accidentals.* In musical notation they are placed to the left
of the notes they modify.

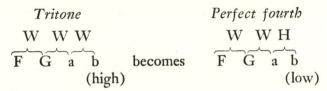

The tritone is not really eliminated from the scale when the alternate b-flat is used. In fact, the tritone will always be present in
diatonic material, and the most that can be done is to shift its position. In this case, the new tritone is formed between b♭ and E, or
b♭ and e. These intervals must be avoided as well as the inversion
B-F of the original tritone (in chant melody the flat is never used
on the low B).

If the b♭ is used at all, it must be used consistently. Odo says.
"Both b♮ and b♭ may not regularly occur in the same melody." It
is, in other words, always to be treated as an alternate, not an ad
ditional tone in the gamut.

The alteration of b is most apt to occur in Modes I, II, V, and VI.
In Modes III or IV it involves possible conflict with the final E. In

---

* The introduction of b♭ as an optional tone along with GG which was added
in the chart of clefs on page 26 completes the medieval gamut approximated by
the order of tones given in Chapter 1.

Modes VII and VIII it changes the step patterns to forms identical with those of Modes I and II.

Having more than one mode with the same step pattern would be against the nature of the modal system, as one of its principal characteristics is variety in this respect. Also, it is unnecessary to write the same pattern starting from different points, as unaccompanied modal melodies can be sung beginning on any comfortable pitch, regardless of the notation. The modes retain their identities, not by the absolute pitches of the starting notes, but by the patterns of steps and the positions of the dominants and the highest and lowest tones in relation to the final.

The following rule pertains to the use of the b-flat, and the avoidance of tritone groupings in chant melody:

> RULE 5. *Use b-flat to avoid conspicuous F-b tritone groupings in Modes I, II, V, and VI. Be careful in doing so not to form other tritone groupings between b-flat and E, or b-flat and e. In Modes III, IV, VII, and VIII (and in cases involving the low B) avoid using the flat, changing the melody in other ways to prevent tritone groupings.*

DECLAMATION

In the Gregorian chant literature we can recognize three distinct kinds of *declamation* (word-setting). One kind is called *syllabic*, since it uses a single note to each syllable. Here is an example (see the complete melody on page 133):

O   come, O   come Em - man -   u - el

When there are many instances of two or three notes to a syllable, as on the word "Emmanuel" in the above example, the declamation is called *grouped*. Here is a phrase in *grouped style* (complete melody on page 136):

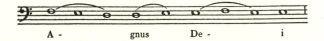

A -   gnus   De -   i

A passage with more than three or four notes to one syllable is called a *melisma*. The following phrase is from a melody which is in *melismatic style*, since it contains a number of phrases like the one shown here on the syllable "e" (complete melody on page 134):

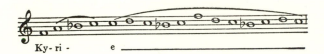

Ky- ri -   e _____

FORM

The chant literature offers us clear examples of three basic approaches to the element of repetition, which is vitally important in crystallizing the form of a piece of music. In the first approach, the absence of repetition and the emphasis on freely unfolding patterns are most characteristic. In the second, the repetitions occur only with small fragments of melody, which we may call *motives*, and in no particular order. In the third, the repetitions are of fairly large units of melody, which set up noticeable symmetries of various kinds. The patterns produced by the latter type can be symbolized by letters, and in this way formal schemes may be diagrammed. For example, the order of the sections might be A-B-A, or A-A-B-A, or any others of an infinite number of possibilities. In the actual literature these three types seldom occur in pure form, but usually in some kind of mixture. There is no compulsion, of course, for the patterns of repetition in the music to follow those of the text, although this is often the case. The examples given at the end of this chapter (pages 132 through 135) illustrate the three basic approaches to the element of repetition, and show various relationships between musical and textual form.

CHANT MELODIES: NOTATION, PROCEDURE

Although there is a complete and very subtle system of notation for Gregorian chant, we shall not attempt to use it for our own melodies. It has little actual connection with modern notation, and it would lead us into a specialized study that would be quite unnecessary for our present needs. The following method is a temporary adaptation designed simply to carry us over the immediate demands of unmeasured modal melody:

1. Use treble or bass clef. When men use the treble clef, they may indicate that the sounds are an octave lower by the following modified treble clef: *

When women use the bass clef, they may show that the sounds are an octave higher by this modified bass clef:

2. Write the melodies mostly in whole-notes, which will be assumed to move in flowing style (two or three whole-notes to about 80 on the metronome). The notes should be rather even, with deviations only on single isolated notes. These might be:

   a. A note shorter than normal, shown by a black note without stem.

   b. A note of approximately double value, shown by two whole-notes tied together.

* Two other modified clefs with the same meaning, which are found in the tenor parts of some editions of choral music, are:

     and

(c clef on the third space)

c. A note of triple value, shown by three whole-notes tied together.

The notes which are shorter and longer than normal should seldom be used (especially the triple-length note), and never in an order tending to establish a definite meter. Since beginning or ending slowly may be taken for granted in the manner of performance, these exceptional notes should not begin or end sections.

Accentuation for these settings had best come from the text, although (as examples will show) this is not easily demonstrable in authentic chant literature.

3. When each syllable in a word gets a separate note, hyphenate the syllables, placing each one under its proper tone.

(For the proper division of words, consult a good dictionary.)

When one syllable gets more than one note, place a slur over the notes.

A broken line separates the syllables in these cases, unless the extension comes at the end of a word, as in the example below:

Here a solid line is used.

4. Show breathing and phrasing by different bar-lines. A very short breath (in the middle of a phrase, or even in the course of a very long melisma) is shown by a line drawn through the top two spaces. A full breath, at the end of a phrase, is shown by a single line drawn all the way through the staff. Sectional endings are shown by a double line drawn completely through the staff. The end of a piece is shown by a double line, one of which is thickened.

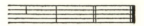

5. In these melodies the flat is added to the b each time it is needed. Its validity will not be assumed to carry over from one b to another.

For the texts of our melodic experiments we shall use psalms. They are ideally appropriate for the purpose since psalm-singing was one of the first forms of the historical chant, and since the psalm texts are so suggestive in mood and clear in structural implication.

The texts given here are from the King James Version of the Bible. Any other version may be used, if desired.

The actual procedure for writing a chant-setting should be:

1. Read the text in order to find in it any evidences of parallelism which might be helpful in determining the form of the melody. Decide (whether the text provides formal suggestions or not) on the manner in which repetition will be employed as a means of organizing the melody.

2. Decide what style of declamation is most appropriate to the text. Melismas tend to emphasize words. Therefore try to place them where the expressive meaning justifies such emphasis.

3. Determine the mode to be used, and review all the conditions of range and ending formulas that pertain to it.

4. After a thorough study of the text, and advance planning for the details of form, style, and mode, try to sing a melody extemporaneously. It will be best to write nothing down on paper until your musical impulse has crystallized into a melodic contour for the opening phrase which is definite enough for you to remember

and repeat several times without variation. After writing down the opening phrase, repeat this process with the other phrases, singing first, and then writing.

Needless to say, the aural image of all the intervals must be fixed at this stage so that the melody as imagined and sung will take the correct form when notated. If necessary, though, use the piano as a means of checking to see if your written and sung versions really agree.

EXPERIMENT 40.

a. Set the following texts in chant style according to the procedures given above.

b. Set any longer psalm texts of your own choice.

c. Use the psalm settings to be composed here for sight-reading and for dictation practice.

TEXTS FOR CHANT MELODY

Text 1. Psalm 61, 1.

"Hear my cry, O God; attend unto my prayer."

Text 2. Psalm 81, 1.

"Sing aloud unto God our strength: make a joyful noise unto the God of Jacob."

Text 3. Psalm 62, 1.

"Truly my soul waiteth upon God: from him cometh my salvation."

Text 4. Psalm 83, 1.

"Keep not thou silence, O God: hold not thy peace, and be not still, O God."

The following texts, which are somewhat longer, offer more possibilities for formal planning.

Text 5. Psalm 42, 1 and 2.

"As the hart panteth after the water brooks, so panteth my soul after thee, O God."

2. "My soul thirsteth for God, for the living God: when shall I come and appear before God?"

Text 6. Psalm 130, 1 and 2.

"Out of the depths have I cried unto thee, O Lord."

2. "Lord, hear my voice: let thine ears be attentive to the voice of my supplications."

Text 7. Psalm 84, 1 and 2.

"How amiable are thy tabernacles, O Lord of hosts!"

2. "My soul longeth, yea, even fainteth for the courts of the Lord: my heart and my flesh crieth out for the living God."

Text 8. Psalm 96, 1 and 2.

"O sing unto the Lord a new song: sing unto the Lord all the earth."

2. "Sing unto the Lord, bless his name; show forth his salvation from day to day."

MELODY: SOME GENERAL CONSIDERATIONS

The melodies of the above experiment, when completed, should be sung by their composers to the whole classroom group. At this time it will be found that the effects of the melodies vary considerably, even when every one of the rules is scrupulously observed. While the secret of pleasing melody will always be beyond the scope of even the most detailed rules, a few general considerations (relating not only to chant, but to other kinds of melody as well) may be helpful in explaining poor melodic results.

Melodic interest is generally impeded by:

1. Excessive repetitions of the same tone, or groups of two or three tones.

2. Excessive stepwise movement, unrelieved by occasional skips,

or the reverse—excessive skipping, without the relief of stepwise movement.

3. Aimlessness in the conduct of the melodic curve.

This last point, aimlessness, is clearly sensed in an already composed melody; but it is extremely difficult to suggest in advance, with any sort of precision, the proper procedures to prevent it. If we examine melodies of known good effect, we can observe certain features which contribute to that effect, but the transference of these exact features to some other melodic situation could never be guaranteed to give the same good result.

Generally speaking, it is the proper placement of the points of highest intensity which seems to give a line its sense of direction and purpose, and prevents the impression of aimlessness. Sometimes these high points, or climaxes, coincide with expressive elements in the text, such as in Example 2 on page 133 ("Veni Emmanuel") at the words "Rejoice! Rejoice!" Or they may consist of an over-all intensification in an entire section of a piece; the return of the "Kyrie" in the third section of Example 3, page 134, carries the melody to a higher and more intense level after the lower placement of the tones in the "Christe" section.

On the other hand, the absence of such specific climactic points does not make the line of Example 4, page 134 ("Sanctus"), less purposeful or less beautiful than that of the "Kyrie." In this case the curve undulates around a central axis (G).

The fifth example ("Agnus Dei," on page 135) has, however, a wide curve which reaches a significant climax on the tones set to the word *peccata* ("sins").

Even after these few examples, it should begin to be plain that we are dealing with a matter which lies beyond the scope of precise rules. Whether or not the tones go high or low, or remain in the same area, only an essential ingredient which we must describe inadequately as "melodic impulse" can successfully dictate their courses. As the melodies of Experiment 40 are performed in class, it will be possible to observe greater or lesser degrees of this impulse, or motivation. While a general lack of experience with unaccompanied melody may at first somewhat hamper our critical faculties, a set of definite comparative standards will soon emerge.

Aesthetic judgment, then, based on the effects of the melodies as sung, will remain the final test, rather than precise conformity to any rules or principles of construction.

EXPERIMENT 41.

Sing the following examples from chant literature,* and analyze them as to mode, melodic characteristics, treatment of text, and form.

EXAMPLES OF CHANT MELODIES

1. Alleluias. The flavor of each mode is illustrated concisely by the following *alleluias*, which are sung in the Roman service as additions to other chants at Easter.

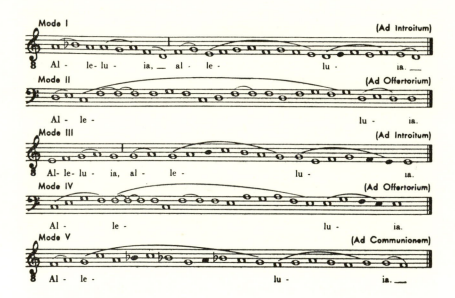

* All of the Gregorian literature in its own regular notation may be found in the official publications of the Roman Catholic Church. The hymn "Veni Emmanuel" may be found with a harmonization, and in modern notation, in the 1940 Hymnal of the Protestant Episcopal Church.

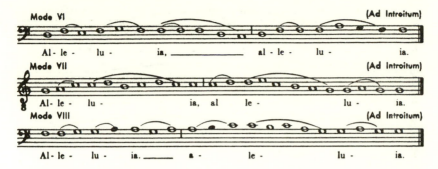

2. "Veni Emmanuel." This famous Advent hymn is an adaptation by Thomas Helmore (1854) from a plainsong melody. It is a clear illustration of Mode I. Note also the use of repetition in the form.

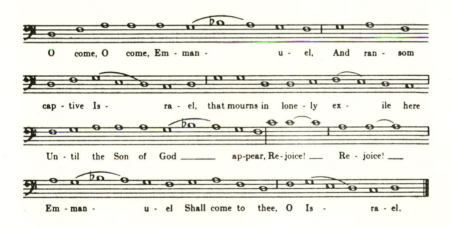

3. "Kyrie" (from the Mass *In Festis Duplicibus* 5). The following chant in Mode V is of late origin (fifteenth or sixteenth century). It will be easier to sing than some of the older chants, and by comparison with them it will have a curiously modern ring. After completing the study of scales and keys in the following chapters, re-examine this melody to see what makes it sound so modern. Note the use of repetition in the form.

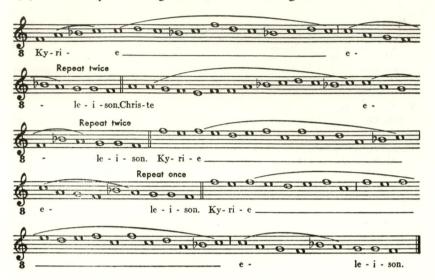

Ky - ri -   e _____   e -

Repeat twice

- le - i -son.Chris-te   e -

Repeat twice

- le - i - son. Ky- ri - e _____

Repeat once

e -   le - i - son. Ky- ri - e _____

_____   e -   le - i - son.

English translation of the Greek text:
    Lord, have mercy upon us. Christ, have mercy upon us.
    Lord, have mercy upon us.

4. "Sanctus" (from the Mass *In Festis Duplicibus 1*). This chant
dates from the eleventh century, and is a clear example of Mode
VIII. The repetition of certain small melodic patterns is particularly
interesting. Analyze the form carefully.

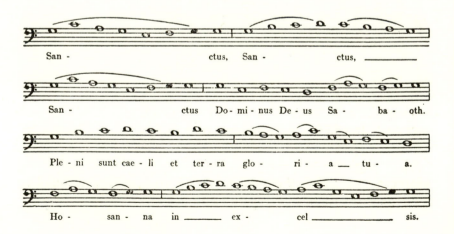

San -   ctus, San -   ctus, _____

San -   ctus Do - mi - nus De - us Sa -   ba - oth.

Ple - ni sunt cae - li et ter - ra glo - ri - a __ tu - a.

Ho -   san - na in _____ ex -   cel _____ sis.

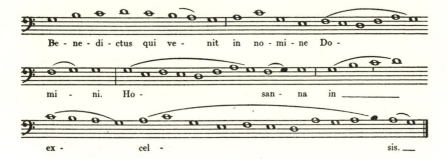

Be - ne - di - ctus qui ve - nit in no - mi - ne Do - mi - ni. Ho - san - na in ex - cel - sis. __

English translation of the Latin text:
Holy, holy, holy, Lord God of Hosts. Heaven and earth are full of Thy glory. Glory be to Thee, O Lord most high. Blessed is he who cometh in the name of the Lord. Glory be to Thee, O Lord most high.

5. "Agnus Dei" (from the Mass *In Festis Solemnibus 2*). The final E is the least used in chant literature. This eleventh- or twelfth-century piece is in the plagal mode on E (IV), with an extension of the range up to d. The text itself has much repetition. Observe how the melodic line follows this pattern of repetition with only slight changes.

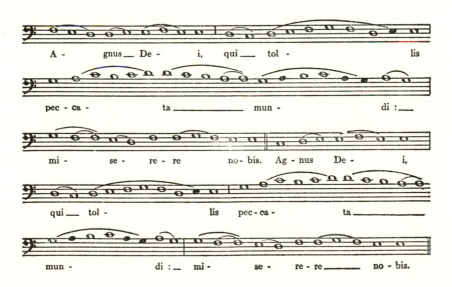

A - gnus __ De - i, qui __ tol - lis pec - ca - ta __ mun - di : __ mi - se - re - re no - bis. Ag - nus De - i, qui __ tol - lis pec - ca - ta __ mun - di : __ mi - se - re - re __ no - bis.

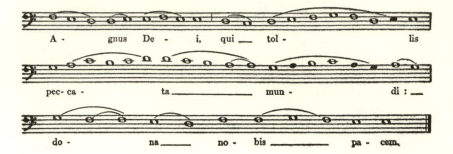

English translation of the Latin text:
O Lamb of God, that takest away the sins of the world, have mercy upon us. O Lamb of God, that takest away the sins of the world, have mercy upon us. O Lamb of God, that takest away the sins of the world, grant us thy peace.

CHAPTER

⚜11⚜

Early Use of Major and Minor Scales. Troubadour and Trouvère Songs

Gregorian chant, as a model, had much to teach us about early methods of tonal organization, the setting of words, melody, and form. The secular melody of medieval France, which was practiced outside the church just when Gregorian art was at its peak, is an equally valuable model. In some ways it was similar to chant, but in other ways it was very much like the familiar music of our own time. Its scales were close to the modes, but contained in essence all the elements of the scales of standard modern usage. Its forms were not unlike those found in some chants, but they were perhaps more like the song forms of comparatively recent traditional literature.

Since French medieval secular melody had characteristics in common with both ancient and more modern practices, it makes an excellent bridge at this point. If we take this music as our next model, we will not lose contact with the knowledge gained from the study of chant, and we will be projected further along toward the theoretical formulations of more recent times.

THE MODEL: MELODIES OF THE TROUBADOURS
AND TROUVÈRES

The melodic literature which is to be our next model was cultivated in medieval France by wandering minstrels, called *jongleurs*, and aristocratic poet-musicians called *troubadours* (southern France) or *trouvères* (northern France).* These men wrote

* An excellent book about them in English is *Trouvères and Troubadours, A Popular Treatise* by Pierre Aubry, translated by C. Aveling (New York: G. Schirmer, 1914).

137

mainly of love and chivalry; since their songs were the flower of their active lives, they themselves had little time to theorize about them. Consequently, there is no treatise on this music by any of its actual composers. And while secular songs are mentioned in some general treatises of the time, there is no one work devoted exclusively to them. We cannot, for this reason, duplicate the procedure of the previous chapter in turning to a contemporary document for already well-formulated principles. But we do have much of the music itself, which has been transcribed from certain large manuscript collections of the medieval period, and we have modern writings about the music, mainly by the scholars who have made the transcriptions. From these two sources (especially the musical examples themselves) we can put together enough information to make experiments in melody-writing in the approximate style of the troubadours and trouvères.

EARLY USE OF THE MAJOR SCALE

The ancient theorist who gives the most information about secular melody (Johannes de Grocheo) makes the statement that the modes of secular music did not conform to the system used in church music. That this was true can be seen by looking at the song, "Main se levoit Aäliz" (Example 5, page 171). This melody is diatonic, and is clearly based on C as the final; this mode was not included among the chant modes, and in fact, was called *modus lascivus* because of its secular associations.

The *modus lascivus* was different from the old chant modes particularly in the way it flaunted half-step progressions into the final in endings. As a residue of ancient pentatonic feeling, the chant modes modestly avoided half-step progressions in endings leading to the final F. But in secular music a more advanced kind of diatonic feeling was in evidence, and such endings were common, both in the new mode on C and in the secular uses of the old mode on F, which, when the b♮ was used, had exactly the same step pattern as the *modus lascivus*. See typical examples of these unchantlike progressions in the endings of the third and fourth phrases of "Main se levoit Aäliz," and in the fifteenth measure of "Amours, cent mille merciz" (Example 2, page 167).

One of the strongest connections between this medieval music and the music of more recent times is found in the use of the scales on C and F (with b♭), which are nothing less than early examples of what we now call the *major scale*.

The major scale gets its name from the interval between the first and third steps, which is a major third.

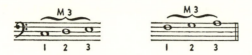

The seventh step of the major scale, which lies a half-step below the upper octave of the final (b-c, or e-f), is called in modern usage a *leading tone*, because it directs the ear with such smoothness into the final.

The consistent use of b♭ in the scale on F to avoid the tritone between the first and fourth steps shows a stronger feeling for interval relationships than was always characteristic of the modes. The major scales of secular usage always had tones which made the strong intervals of a perfect fourth and a perfect fifth above the final.

The various characteristics of the major scale are shown in the following diagram:

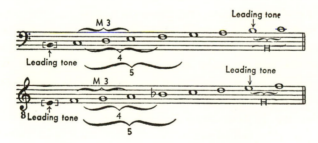

Characteristics of the Major Scale

EXPERIMENT 42.

a. Diagram the whole- and half-step patterns of the major scales on C and F, as on page 104, Chapter 9.

1. C   D   E   F   G   a   b   c

2. F   G   a   b♭   c   d   e   f

b. Play these scales on the piano, and sing them.

c. Sing major scales starting on tones other than C or F (i.e., starting on any convenient pitches).

The church mode on G also had a major third (G-B), but the tone below the final was a whole-step away (F-G). The secular taste of the medieval period was so conditioned by the *modus lascivus* that when the mode on G was used, the F was altered in endings to produce a leading tone. A form of the square b (similar to the ♮) was used to indicate this alteration. The modern sign which we use for the same purpose is likewise a derivation of the ancient square b. It is called a *sharp* (symbol: ♯), and when placed to the left of a note, it raises the pitch by a half-step. Like the flat, the sharp may be canceled by a natural.

The mode on G does not, through this alteration at ending points, become a real major scale like those on C and F; it becomes what we may best term an "altered" mode. Such alterations, called *musica falsa* in the thirteenth century, are described by theorists of the time, but are not actually written in the manuscripts with the consistency we would expect. It is assumed that they were often added in performance, even though they were not always written down. Because of the casual treatment of the accidentals in the manuscripts, all modern transcribers have their difficulties in deciding where to alter and where not to alter. Such a case is the song, "Por conforter ma pesance" (Example 1, page 167). The transcriber believes the F before the end should be raised, although he omits another possibility at the words "le taisson."

EARLY USE OF THE MINOR SCALE

The feeling for leading tones in secular music was not confined to the modes with the major thirds; it applied also to the mode on D, which had a minor third. The seventh tone of this mode (or the tone below the final) was raised in endings from c to c♯.

While the occasional alteration of the f to f♯ in the mode on G is not enough to qualify it as a real major scale in the modern sense, the occasional alteration of the c to c♯ in the mode on D does give this mode the form of the present-day scale called the *melodic minor*. Any diatonic scale with a minor third could be called a "minor scale," and music theory acknowledges several of them.* This particular one is called the "melodic" minor because its shape resulted from a requirement of melody (the need for a leading tone). Since melody requires the leading tone mainly in ascending progressions to the final, the raised seventh step is shown only in ascending. In descending, the c becomes natural again, and the sixth step is lowered from b to b♭. The latter alteration is nothing new, since even in the chant mode on D there were optional forms for the b. The complete melodic minor scale on D therefore assumes the following form:

Melodic Minor Scale

EXPERIMENT 43.

a. Diagram the step pattern of the melodic minor scale.

D E F G a b c♯ d c♮ b♭ a G F E D

* Other forms of the minor scale are discussed in Chapter 14, pages 189 through 191.

b. Play this scale on the piano, and sing it.

c. Sing other melodic minor scales, keeping the correct step pattern, but starting on any convenient pitches.

A considerable difference in the characters of the major and minor scales may have been observed. The major scale may have sounded bright and clear, and may have been easy to sing; while the minor scale may have seemed somewhat darker and more difficult. Some of this difference in character can be attributed to the third steps of the scales, by which they were given the designations "major" and "minor." But in the modal system there were differences in the third steps (those of the modes on D and E were minor, while those on F and G were major), and still no such marked contrast in effect was evident. The real reasons for the differences in major and minor scales lie more in the alterations which transform the old mode with a minor third into a minor scale than in the quality of the thirds. The significant fact is that these alterations bring in nondiatonic elements; chromaticism is mainly what accounts for the darkness and complexity of the minor scale. And to explain adequately why this is the case, we must now embark on an independent discussion of the problems of chromaticism, returning afterward to the details of writing melodies in troubadour-trouvère style.

⚜12⚜

Chromaticism

In the generalized discussion of the chromatic order in Chapter 9 (page 102) it was pointed out that the expression of chromaticism does not require all twelve notes of the chromatic scale, and that small groups of tones can be chromatic simply by violating the essential conditions of diatonicism. That discussion also promised a more positive definition of chromaticism at a later stage. The minor scale and our increased knowledge of accidentals now bring us to that stage.

CHROMATICISM IN THE MINOR SCALE

The ascending form of the melodic minor scale contains the following tonal groups which violate the pattern of the diatonic order,* and are therefore chromatic: (1) two half-steps within the space of a fourth; (2) two different tritones within the octave.

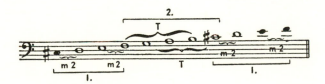

Aside from the new and complex chromatic sound of these tonal groups, some new problems of notation and interval terminology are brought forward by this example. We shall discuss these problems first, and return later to the actual sounding element of chromaticism

---

* By the simple test given earlier these groups may be proved chromatic: they cannot be found at any point among the white keys.

which produces them. The notation and terminology problems here are not themselves chromaticism; they are merely symptomatic disturbances produced by the injection of chromatic elements into a notation system which was designed for diatonicism.

CHROMATIC INTERVALS: ENHARMONIC SPELLING

The outer tones of the chromatic groups enclosed by the square brackets in the previous diagram form chromatically spelled intervals.

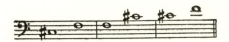

These intervals have the appearance of fourths and fifths, but the accidentals change them so that in actual size they are equivalent to thirds and sixths. For instance, the two that look like fourths span the correct number of staff lines and spaces, and involve four letter names (C♯, D, E, and F); but counting their sizes in half-steps (using both white and black keys) reveals that they are only as large as major thirds. Five white and black keys are required to span the interval from C♯ to F, and these keys have four half-step intervals between them.

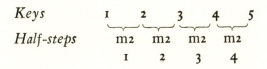

This is the same distance as between C and E, or any other major third.

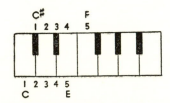

Since the fourth C♯-F is smaller than a perfect fourth, it is called a *diminished fourth*.

The inversion of the diminished fourth, F-c♯, covers nine keys, which have eight half-steps between them.

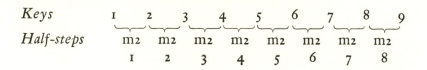

Keys	1	2	3	4	5	6	7	8	9
Half-steps	m2	m2	m2	m2	m2	m2	m2	m2	
	1	2	3	4	5	6	7	8	

This is the same distance as between E and c, or any other minor sixth.

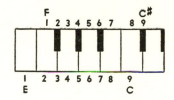

Since the fifth F-c♯ is larger than a perfect fifth, it is called an *augmented fifth*.

Our system of notation has only seven letter names to account for an octave filled with twelve tones, and it does so very well by adding sharps and flats to the letter names. But the spelling of any combinations which involve the black keys (as chromatic groups inevitably do) is complicated by the fact that each black key has two possible meanings: it can be a sharped form of the white key below it, or it can be a flatted form of the one above. Complex spellings also require sharps and flats in the areas B-C and E-F, where no black key comes between the white ones. Here the next higher or lower white key expresses the sharped or flatted tone. The diagram on page 146 shows various spelling for the tones:

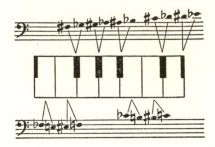

A given sound, then, involving certain keys on the piano, can be written in more than one way. Different spellings of the same sound are called *enharmonic equivalents*. The diminished fourth, for example, is enharmonically equivalent to a major third, and the augmented fifth to a minor sixth. Here are these intervals with some of their enharmonic equivalents:

The major thirds and minor sixths in the above illustration are *not* chromatically spelled intervals, in spite of the sharps and flats. A chromatically spelled interval is distinguished by a disagreement between letter counting and half-step counting (always involving the use of the terms "augmented" and "diminished"), and except when this is the case, the spelling is diatonic. The major third C♯-E♯, for example, spans the correct number of letters for a third (C-D-E),

                                                1 2 3

and is therefore not chromatic. This is likewise true of its inversion E♯-c♯ (E-F-G-a-b-c).

            1 2 3 4 5 6

A consideration of both the ascending and descending forms of the melodic minor scale reveals still more chromatic groupings. All the chromatic tones from A to d are present:

The second line of the above illustration contains two kinds of half-step spellings. The *a-b♭* and *c♯-d* involve two letter names, as minor seconds should in diatonic spelling; they are called *diatonic half-steps*. But b♭-b♮ and c-c♯, while minor seconds in sound, involve only one letter name, and are, therefore, chromatically spelled. In melodic form, these intervals are called *chromatic half-steps,* and in harmonic form, *augmented unisons,* or *augmented primes*.

Between various tones, other chromatically spelled intervals can be found. For example:

The first interval in this illustration involves two letter names (b-c) and is a second, but the flat on b and the sharp on the c make the interval as large (in half-steps) as a minor third. Therefore, it is called an *augmented second*. Its inversion, b♭-C♯, has the appearance of a seventh, but both of the accidentals tend to contract the interval—the sharp upward and the flat downward—and its actual size is only that of a major sixth. Therefore, it is called a *diminished seventh*.

Certain other large chromatic groups with three or more notes can be formed by the ascending and descending tones.

Three tritones are present:

Characteristic chromatic formations occur, which consist of both a major and minor third above or below a given tone.

We have seen by now how complex the problems of spelling and terminology can become when chromatic elements enter our diatonically designed notation. We can summarize this problem, as far as intervals are concerned, by the following chart, which may also help to make clear the use of the terms "augmented" and "diminished."

DIATONIC AND CHROMATIC INTERVALS.
ENHARMONIC EQUIVALENTS

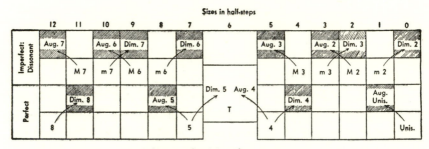

Light squares: diatonic intervals
Darkened squares: chromatic intervals
Arrows to the right point to diminished forms of intervals.
Arrows to the left point to augmented forms of intervals.

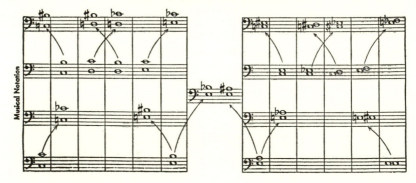

EXPERIMENT 44.

a. Name the following intervals, and write under each one a diatonically spelled enharmonic equivalent:

b. Write chromatically spelled enharmonic equivalents of the diatonic intervals given in the chart of Experiment 19, page 28.

CHROMATIC FORMULAS

The term "chromatic interval" used at the top of the chart on page 148, and often used in musical terminology elsewhere, is really a casual inaccuracy. "Chromatically spelled interval" is a clumsier but more accurate designation, for, actually, two notes alone are incapable of producing a sound which clearly expresses the chromatic order. If we hear (but do not see) any two-note combinations, we automatically assume that they are the normal intervals. One or two more tones together with these are necessary to establish a real chromatic context. When such a context is established, the individual intervals themselves undergo certain changes in intonation (if not performed on an instrument with fixed pitches like the piano or the organ), and an element of uncertainty enters as to the locations and functions of the tones. This element of uncertainty shows itself when we attempt to sing real chromatic groupings; we will usually lack the clear pre-image of the sounds (especially when wide leaps are involved) which is essential to producing a tone with the voice. Of course, the ability to cope with chromatic problems may be acquired to some extent. But in most cases what brings a singer through a melody of this kind is either a memory for the anonymous sounds of the keyboard (on which the same notes can be sharps or flats), or a strong feeling for separate intervals which makes it possible to crawl along the melody chain without attempting to relate the separate links to the whole. Using the latter method, try to sing the following chromatic successions without the help of a piano.

In the tonal groups of the illustration below only major thirds and minor sixths (by half-step counting) are employed, but the chromaticism inherent in the groups forces chromatic spellings. Since the separate intervals are easy, one might think the examples should be easy to sing. But a practical proof of the chromatic context is that they are not easy, in spite of the simplicity of the individual intervals.

Here below is a still more complicated example, but if the intervals of the first chapter were thoroughly learned it should nevertheless be possible to sing it. It is again the influence of the chromatic order, rather than the individual interval leaps, that accounts for the difficulty.

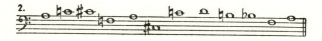

While singing one tritone in a diatonic scale was not always easy, several of them in a melodic line greatly intensify the difficulty:

Half-steps in succession are easy to sing even though chromatic because the voice has very little effort to make in getting from one note to the next. But when these progressions are inverted or expanded so that the half-steps become sevenths and ninths, they form one of the most difficult kinds of chromatic melody.

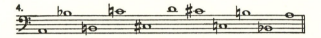

If we concern ourselves with interval groupings and actual sounds, and ignore the many possible spellings, all chromaticism can be reduced to four typical formulas. One or more of these formulas will be present in every chromatic situation. Each of the four preceding examples featured one of them. The formulas are:

1. *Two superimposed major thirds* (symbol: MM), in Example 1 on page 150 shown by these tones:

2. *A major and minor third above or below a given tone* (symbol: Mm), in Example 2 on page 150, shown by these tones:

3. *Two or more different tritones within an octave* (symbol: TT). In Example 3, above, shown by these tones, in a different order:

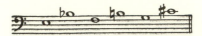

4. *Two or more half-steps within a fourth* (symbol: HH). In Example 4, page 151, this is shown by any consecutive combination of three or more tones:

The above formulas give us, at last, the positive definition of chromaticism which was promised earlier. A re-examination of the melodic minor scale in the light of this definition will indicate now the exact extent of its chromaticism. In the following diagram the chromatic formulas are singled out and identified by the symbols used above.

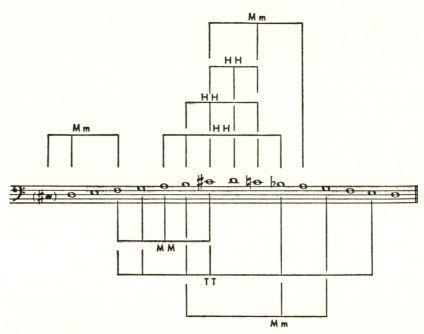

CHROMATIC FORMULAS IN THE MELODIC MINOR SCALE

EXPERIMENT 45.

Look again at the Schoenberg melodies given at the end of Chapter 9 (page 113). See how many chromatic formulas you can single out in the melodic lines.

The student may well ask, after this exploration of chromaticism, why it is necessary for him to face all these complications now. Wouldn't it suffice for him to wait until he is ready to write a chromatic melody to consider all this? If he never expects to arrive at that point, is there any purpose now in his worrying about these things?

The purpose in discussing chromaticism at this early stage is not to teach the student how to compose chromatic melodies, but to help him understand more fully at later stages the many rules of traditional theory which are directed toward the *control* of chromaticism. As we have seen, even the ordinary melodic minor scale contains chromatic elements, and rules have to be devised which direct the use of these elements so that they do not destroy their essentially diatonic environment. These rules will be necessary even for the melodies of Chapter 13, and will increase in number as we proceed further into the study of traditional theory.

To the chant-singing monks of the Middle Ages, the one tritone found in each mode was *"diabolus in musica."* Their sensibilities, still more or less on the pentatonic level, were offended by the sound of the tritone; but since its presence could not be avoided if the full supply of seven tones to the octave were to be utilized, they simply dodged it, and avoided melodic formations which gave it undue prominence. The subsequent development of music has removed the early stigma from the tritone, but the role of the "devil in music" has been passed along to chromaticism. How to utilize the full supply of twelve tones without the consequent possible loss of tonal security and clarity is one of the major problems of contemporary theory.

CHAPTER
⚔ 13 ⚔
Melody-Writing Modeled on Troubadour and Trouvère Songs

After the necessary discussion in Chapter 12 of the elements of chromaticism as they appear in the melodic minor scale, we must return to the specific problem at hand—the scales to be used in composing melodies similar to those of the troubadours and trouvères.

SCALES FOR SECULAR MELODIES

We have already seen that there were in French medieval secular melody two regular major scales (C and F), another semimodal scale on G with an optional f♯, and a melodic minor scale on D. All we need to complete this scale system is another melodic minor scale on *a*, with the same step pattern as the one on D.

EXPERIMENT 46.

Add the necessary accidentals to the following scale to give it a step pattern identical with that of the melodic minor scale on D:

A comparison between these secular scales and the church modes will reveal the following differences:

1. There are two new finals (C and *a*), but the final E is missing. The final E was less commonly used than any of the others even in chant melody, and in secular music it was practically nonexistent. The new strong feeling for the leading tone moving upward by a half-step into the final may have turned attention from this mode, which has the opposite—a low second step as a leading tone progressing downward to the final (F-E).

2. While there are five finals (C, D, F, G, and *a*), the secular system is less varied than the church modes, because C and F, and D and *a*, have identical step patterns. Also, in these melodies, no organized distinction is made with regard to range; there are no clearly defined authentic and plagal forms of these scales.

Here, for easy reference, is a chart of the scales to be used in this chapter:

Scales for Secular Melodies

Major

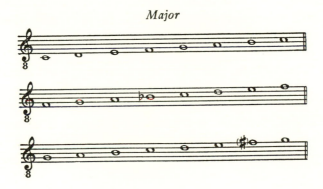

Minor

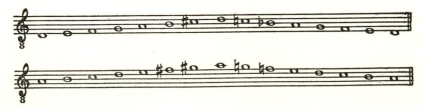

MELODIC MOTION

The following rules will guide us in writing melodic lines similar to those of the troubadours and trouvères:

1. The tonal material will consist of the five scales shown above: major scales on C, F, and G, and minor scales on D and *a*.

2. The ranges of the melodies should span approximately an octave.

3. The treatment of leaps will be similar to that in chant melody: no leaps of a tritone, and none larger than a fifth.

4. Melodies may start on the final, or occasionally on some other tone.

5. Melodies must end on the final, although sectional endings may occur on other tones. All endings should be approached smoothly (i.e., stepwise, or by small leaps), but there are no specific restrictions in this regard.

6. The high sixth steps and leading tones of the minor scales, and the f♯ in the scale on G are to be used only in melodic lines which are directed upward toward the final. In lines with descending tendencies, the low forms of these tones are to be used.

7. As in chant melody, all obvious tritone formations are to be avoided. This includes not only those formed around F and b, but also the new tritone possibilities brought in by the minor scales.

8. The chromatically related tones of the minor scales must be kept sufficiently far apart to conceal the presence of chromaticism. Fairly close chromatic relations (less than three or four notes apart) may be possible only when the tones are separated by clear phrase endings.

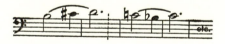

No direct chromatic progressions are possible, such as:

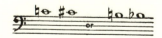

Chromatic leaps of all kinds are to be avoided:

No larger melodic group containing any of the four previously given chromatic formulas is to be used.

RHYTHM

Written French secular melody looks very much like chant. It used the same sort of notation, which showed the pitches of the tones, but not their exact durations. However, there is evidence to suggest that these pieces were actually sung with more feeling of measured rhythm than chant, and modern scholars have tried to determine what this rhythm was. While it seems that no two scholars ever arrive at exactly the same result when transcribing the same piece, most of them agree that the rhythm of secular songs depended on the application (in performance, not in notation) of certain *rhythmic modes*.

The rhythmic modes were patterns similar to ancient Greek poetic feet. Although we do not know exactly how they were placed in duple or triple metrical groupings, we do know the relative proportions of the patterns. Those most commonly used were:

1. *Trochaic:* long-short.
2. *Iambic:* short-long.
3. *Dactylic:* long-short-short.

Rather than define the rhythmical style to be used in this chapter according to the abstract terminology developed in Part I, we can rely on these rhythmic modes to keep us within simple and appropriate boundaries. This does not mean that the pieces we shall write will be restricted to lengthy successions of long-short or short-long patterns; there are enough ways of elaborating the patterns to prevent that dull result. But the patterns will serve as skeletons for the rhythmical structure, and they will help to establish a connection between the poetic and musical meters.

We shall place the first two modes (trochaic and iambic) in triple meter, using bars of $\frac{3}{8}$, $\frac{3}{4}$, or $\frac{3}{2}$. Each modal pattern will fill one bar.

For the sake of variety, we shall place the dactylic mode in duple meter, using bars of $\frac{2}{8}$, $\frac{2}{4}$, or $\frac{2}{2}$.*

Variety may be achieved within the structure of the modal patterns by:

1. Using one long note for the whole bar in endings.
2. Filling out the long note of the basic pattern. For example:

Occasionally the filling-out may consist of faster notes (second division), or simple foreign patterns.

* An example of the scholarly conflict over the rhythm of this music is that one authority (Jean Beck) says that the dactylic mode should be expressed in duple rhythm, as given here, while another authority (Pierre Aubry) says it should be in triple rhythm ($\frac{6}{4}$ ♩. ♩ ♪).

3. Omission of the short note in trochaic, or the two short notes in dactylic. For example:

FORMS

While many chant melodies were organized by small motives which occur in such subtle placements as to make schematic diagrams of the forms very difficult, the secular melodies were organized in larger and more easily definable sections, which can be shown very well in diagrams. This was no doubt partly because the poetry itself was organized in definite and well-defined schemes.

From the various fixed forms of French medieval secular music we shall select several types which bear close resemblances to the song and instrumental forms of more modern practice. In naming these forms, however, we run into certain difficulties: in some instances the same form had different names in northern and southern France, and in other cases no name at all was given by the composers themselves. Names have been applied by modern scholars to all of the types, but, just as in the case of the rhythmic modes, not without dispute. For our purposes it will suffice to call one form *chanson* (the modern French word for "song") which we will recognize in two varieties—*simple* and *rounded*. The other form we shall use is the *rondeau*. This is the French word for the same type of form which we encounter on a much enlarged scale later on in the "rondo" of such composers as Haydn and Mozart. Here are descriptions of these three forms:

1. *Simple Chanson.* The musical design is A-A-B. The same musical phrase (A) is repeated, although the text contains no repetition. The B section is a new musical phrase set to the remaining lines of the text. See Examples 1, 2, and 3, on pages 167 and 169.

2. *Rounded Chanson.* This form is as above, except that a musical reminiscence of A occurs at the end of the piece (A-A-B-a). See Example 4, page 170. Example 3, page 169, is a borderline case, perhaps not quite qualifying as a rounded chanson, but nevertheless containing a slight reminiscence.

3. *Rondeau.* This form is characterized by a recurring phrase with the same words and music, called a *refrain*. In its original form the refrain was probably sung by a group of people, perhaps those listening to the song. The phrases between refrains were probably sung by a soloist. The solo phrases had different words, but *the tune was the same as that of the refrain*. Each new solo phrase carried the narrative forward between the persistent and repetitious exclamations (refrains) of the choral group.

In simpler pieces the music sometimes consists of one phrase repeated over and over, almost without change, as the text unfolds. See Example 5, page 171.

In larger pieces the musical phrase itself may have two or three elements (A-B, or A-B-C). Much variety is obtained by the occasional omission of the second or third elements. See Examples 6 and 7, pages 171 and 172.

SECULAR MELODIES: NOTATION, PROCEDURE

The melody-writing projects of this chapter bring in certain new aspects of notation. One of them concerns the validity of accidentals within bars, and the other has to do with the treatment of beams in vocal music. (The regulating principles for these matters, as stated below, apply generally—not only in this particular chapter.)

1. An accidental is valid through the whole measure in which it occurs, unless it is canceled by a natural.

An accidental given in one octave does not affect the same note in another octave, even when both tones occur in the same measure. In such cases the accidental has to be repeated.

2. Beams in measured vocal music are usually adjusted to show the distribution of syllables. Notes which would be joined by beams in instrumental music are written with separate stems if attached to separate syllables.

While the usual beaming may be broken down into smaller groups to go with the distribution of short syllables, long syllables do not indicate the connection of normal beams into unreadable long groups.

Here is the procedure for setting to music the translated French poems which are given below (pages 163–165). The principal new problem with these settings (as contrasted to chant) will be the coordination of the musical and textual accents.

1. Go through the text and mark the accented syllables. For example:

>   >   >   >   >
"Breath-ing do I draw that air to me"

Each accent, according to your reading, should coincide with the metric accent of the musical meter you employ. The metric accent in the simple meters we are to use here can only be the first beat of the bar. The above line could be set in the trochaic mode as follows:

Breath - ing   do   I   draw   that   air   to   me

The second line of this poem (Text No. 1, page 164) is less regular, but it could be set musically in several ways, according to the choice of stresses. For instance:

Which   I   feel   com - ing   from   Pro - ven - ça

Which I   feel com - ing   from Pro - ven - ça

Which I   feel   com - ing   from   Pro -   ven - ça

What must be strictly avoided is the placement of unaccented syllables on the metric accents, as in the example below:

Which   I   feel   com - ing   from   Pro - ven -   ça

2. After marking the accents, decide the rhythmic mode, and write the whole rhythmic structure for the piece in pencil, lightly, above the staff. Remember that strictly syllabic declamation is unnecessary; some groups and short melismas should be employed. Mark the bars in the actual positions they will occupy on the staff. The preliminary sketch should look something like this:

Soft - ly sighs the A - pril air

3. Decide which of the secular scales you will use, and think over the purely melodic aspects of the setting, as you did with unmeasured chant. Plan the sectional endings in advance. Endings on tones other than the final are "open," and those on the final are "closed." The meaning of the text will often indicate which type of ending is more appropriate. Sometimes, however, it may be desirable to treat a repeated phrase with an open ending at one point, and a closed ending at another.

4. Complete the setting by adding tones in the rhythm indicated above the staff.

Here are translations of some old French song texts which are in the forms we wish to use. The brackets in the margins next to the poems will show how the forms are laid out. Whatever small changes in rhythm these poems may have undergone in translation, their formal schemes remain perfectly clear, and resemble very closely those of the examples in French, given together with their original melodies on pages 166–173. Compare these translated poems with the French examples before you start to make your own settings.

EXPERIMENT 47.

a. Set the following texts in the style of medieval French secular melody, as described above.

b. Use the melodies after they have been completed for sight-singing and dictation practice.

TEXTS FOR SECULAR MELODY

1. Chanson. Peire Vidal (twelfth century), translated by Ezra Pound. Set this text in the form of a simple chanson, according to the brackets placed in the margin.

A {Breathing do I draw that air to me
{Which I feel coming from Provença,

A {All that is thence so pleasureth me
{That whenever I hear good speech of it

B {I listen a-laughing and straightway
{Demand for each word an hundred more,
{So fair to me is the hearing.

2. Chanson. Bertran de Born (twelfth century), translated by Ezra Pound. Set this text also as a simple chanson.

"Song of Battle"

A {Well pleaseth me the sweet time of Easter
{That maketh the leaf and the flower come out.

A {And it pleaseth me when I hear the clamor
{Of the birds' bruit about their song through the wood;

B {And it pleaseth me when I see through the meadows
{The tents and pavilions set up, and great joy have I
{When I see o'er the campana knights armed
{   and horses arrayed.

3. Chanson. Arnaut Daniel (twelfth century), translated by Harriet Waters Preston. Set this text in the form of a rounded chanson, as indicated in the margin.

"Bel m'es quan lo vens m'alena"

A {Softly sighs the April air,
{Ere the coming of the May;

A {Of the tranquil night aware,
{Murmur nightingale and jay;

B {Then, when dewy dawn doth rise,
{Every bird in his own tongue
{Wakes his mate with happy cries;

a   All their joy abroad is flung.

4. Rondeau. Charles d'Orleans (1391–1465), translated by Andrew Lang. The following text will fit the typical scheme for a rondeau given above. The last b is shortened, and the text is modified in the final refrain.

Refrain
- A Strengthen, my Love, this castle of my heart,
- A And with some store of pleasure give me aid,
- B For jealousy, with all them of his part,
- B Strong siege about the weary tower has laid.

a
- Nay, if to break his bands thou art afraid,
- Too weak to make his cruel force depart,

Refrain A
- Strengthen at least this castle of my heart,
- And with some store of pleasure give me aid.

a
- Nay, let not jealousy, for all his art
- Be master, and the tower in ruin laid,

b That still, ah, Love, thy gracious rule obeyed.

Refrain A
- Advance, and give me succor of thy part;
- Strengthen, my Love, this castle of my heart.

5. Rondeau. Jean Froissart (1337–1404), translated by Henry Wadsworth Longfellow. This text is like the preceding one, except that the second refrain and final refrain both consist of A-B in complete form.

Refrain
- A Love, love, what wilt thou with this heart of mine?
- B Naught see I fixed or sure in thee!

a I do not know thee,—nor what deeds are thine:

Refrain
- A Love, love, what wilt thou with this heart of mine?
- B Naught see I fixed or sure in thee!

a Shall I be mute, or vows with prayers combine?

b Ye who are blessed in loving, tell it me:

Refrain
- A Love, love, what wilt thou with this heart of mine?
- B Naught see I permanent or sure in thee!

EXAMPLES OF TROUBADOUR AND TROUVÈRE MELODIES

The following examples from the actual literature will illustrate the three forms used in Experiment 47. The French texts given before each example have form diagrams in the margins for direct comparison with the previously given translated texts, which had similar form diagrams. Next to each of the French texts is a more or less literal English translation. Under the music are free English versions, intended to make the melodies more accessible for singing.

The pieces given here are taken from three of the most important modern scholarly works dealing with the music of the troubadours and trouvères:

1. *Le Chansonnier de l'Arsenal,* transcribed by Pierre Aubry. Societé des anciens textes français, 1909–   .

2. *Le Chansonniers des Troubadours et des Trouvères* (Chansonniers Cangé). Jean Beck. University of Pennsylvania Press, 1927.

3. *Rondeaux, Virelais und Balladen,* Vol. 1. Friedrich Gennrich. Halle: Max Niemeyer Verlag, 1921.

Some details of notation in these various editions (use of slurs, etc.) have been adjusted slightly for consistency, and to conform to the style used in this text. A few other minor deviations from the original transcriptions are mentioned in the paragraphs above the songs in which they occur.

EXPERIMENT 48.

Sing and play the following troubadour and trouvère pieces, noting especially the treatment of form. Also, analyze them as to scale, or mode.

1. Chanson. Thibaut, King of Navarre, transcribed by Aubry. This example perfectly illustrates the form A-A-B. The sharp on the F at the end of the piece is suggested by the transcriber, in keeping with the practice of the time.

A	Por conforter ma pesance	To comfort my grief
	Faz un son:	I shall write a song:
A	Bon est se il m'en avance,	It is good if it advances my cause [with my lady],
	Car Jason,	For [even] Jason
B	Cil qui conquist le taisson,	—He who captured the golden fleece—
	N'ot pas si grief penitence.	Had not such grievous punishment.
	E! E! E! E!	Alas! alas! alas!

No. 1

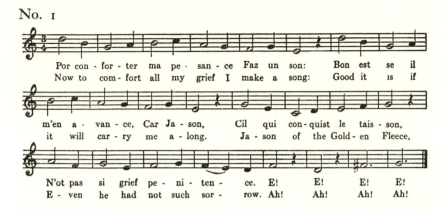

Por con - for - ter ma pe · san - ce Faz un son: Bon est se il
Now to com - fort all my grief I make a song: Good it is if

m'en a · van - ce, Car Ja - son, Cil qui con - quist le tais - son,
it will car - ry me a · long. Ja - son of the Gold - en Fleece,

N'ot pas si grief pe - ni - ten - ce. E! E! E! E!
E - ven he had not such sor - row. Ah! Ah! Ah! Ah!

2. Chanson. Jehannot de L'Escurel, transcribed by Gennrich. Another example of the A-A-B form. Notice the difference in the endings of the A sections. The first one is open, the second one closed.

A 〔 Amours, cent mille merciz   Love, a hundred thousand thanks
   〔 de l'oneur que par vous ai;   For the honor I have had through you;

A 〔 quar j'aim et sui vrais amis,   For I love and am a true lover,
   〔 et sui amé, bien le sai,   And I am loved, I know it well,

   〔 de belle et bonne au cuer vrai   By a fair and good woman with a true heart
B 〔
   │ et telle, qu'a droit jugier,   And such, that judging rightly,
   〔 je ne puis mieux souhaidier.   I couldn't ask for any better.

No. 2

A - mours,_____ cent mil - le mer - ciz
O Love,_____ hun - dred_____ thanks most_ kind,

de l'o - neur_____ que par_____ vous ai;
For the_____ hon - or known_____ through _ you;

quar j'aim _____ et sui _____ vrais a - mis,
For I _____ love, love _____ pure of _ mind,

et   sui ___   a -   mé,   bien ___   le ___   sai,
And   I'm ___   loved, ___   I   al -   ways ___   knew,

de ___   belle   et   bonne   au ___   cuer ___   vrai
By   a   fair   one,   fair ___   and ___   true;

et   tel -   le,   qu'a ___   droit ___   ju -   gier,
Ah!   by   one   that ___   judg -   ing   well,

je   ne ___   puis   mieux   soü -   hai -   dier.
None   could ___   ere   hope ___   to ___   ex -   cel.

3. Chanson. Gillebert de Berneville, transcribed by Aubry. This chanson has a suggestion of the A section at the end of B, making it almost a "rounded" chanson.

The accidentals are given by the transcriber to provide leading tones in endings on the final. Aubry's rhythmic interpretation has not been followed strictly here. The pattern which he gives as

has been changed to   .

A	J'ai fet maint vers de chan- çon	I have made many a verse of song.
	Et s'ai mainte fois chanté;	And if I have many times sung,
A	Onques n'en oi guerredon	I have never received recompense
	Nes tant c'on m'en seüst gré.	Nor has anyone been grateful to me for it.
	Mes ja pour ce n'iere faus.	But despite all that I'll not be false.
B	Tos fins et loiax	Discreet and loyal
	M'en irai	I shall go away
	Et serai	And I shall be
	Sages, si m'en retrerai	Reasonable, and I shall cease
	D'amer celi	Loving her
(a)	Ou il n'a point de merci.	In whom there is no compassion.

No. 3

J'ai fet maint vers__ de __ chan - çon   Et s'ai main - te__
I've made songs to __ man - y a verse,   And if I've sung_

fois __ chan - té;   On - ques n'en oi __ guer - re - don
man - y times,   I have gained naught_ for__ my purse;

Nes tant c'on m'en__ se - üst gré.   Mes ja pour ce__
No one's grate - ful__ for__ my rhymes.   Yet for this I'll__

n'ie - re faus.   Tos fins et lo - iax   M'en i - rai
not be - tray;   Lo - yal, far a - way   I shall go,

Et se - rai   Sa - ges, si m'en re - tre - rai D'a -
And shall bow   Thus to rea - son, and__ shall cease From

mer ce - li   Ou il n'a point__ de__ mer - ci.
lov - ing thee,   In whom there's no__ thanks__ for me.

4. Rounded Chanson. Gace Brulé, transcribed by Beck. An un-
mistakable repetition, at the end of the song, of four measures from
the A section (with slight variations) makes this chanson one of the
"rounded" variety.

Beck suggests no accidentals in his transcription. Those shown
here have been added following the same principle as in the Aubry
transcriptions.

A	Quant voi le temps bel et cler	When I see the weather bright and clear
	Ainz que soit noif ne gelée,	Before it snows or freezes,
A	Chant por moi reconforter,	I sing in order to console myself,
	Que trop ai joie obliée.	For too much have I forgotten joy.
B	Mervoille est com puis durer,	It is a marvel that I can bear it,
	Qu'ades bée a moi grever	For the best-loved [creature] in the world
a	Dou monde la mieux amée.	Now desires to wound me.

No. 4

Quant voi le temps bel et_____ cler__ Ainz que_ soit noif__
When I see days clear and_____ bright,_ Ere it_ snows or__

ne ge - lé - e, Chant por moi re - con - for - ter,___
ere it__ freez - es, Sing I to re - lieve my_____ plight, _

Que trop_ ai joie___ o - bli - é - e. Mer - voille_ est com
For I've_ lost, lost__ all that__ pleas - es. That I__ bear it,

puis du - rer_____ Qu'a - des bé - e a_____ moi__ gre -
I have mar - veled, For the best loved one_____ in __ the _

ver Dou mon - de la_ mieux a - mé - e.
world Now de - sires, de - sires to__ wound__ me.

5. Rondeau. From "Le Roman de la Rose ou de Guillaume de Dole," transcribed by Gennrich. This charming little example shows the principle of alternation between soloist and chorus, which was a feature of the rondeau. The soloist's statement is interrupted, and also followed at the end, by the refrain, which is the exclamation of the chorus.

	a	Main se levoit Aäliz,	Alice got up early
Refrain	A	—*Cui lairai ge mes amors?*—	—*To whom shall I leave my love?*—
	a	biau se para et vesti	Beautifully dressed and readied herself
	b	soz la roche Guion.	Under Guyon cliff.
Refrain	A	*Cui lairai ge mes amors,*	*To whom shall I leave my love,*
	B	*amie, s'a vos non?*	*My dear, if not to you?*

No. 5

Main se le - voit A - ä - liz,   Cui lai - rai ge mes __ a - mors?
Ear - ly up rose A - - lice,   Ah! to whom shall I __ give love?

biau se pa - ra et __   ves - ti soz la ro - che __ Gui - on.
Dressed and beaut - i - fied __   her - self Down un - der Cliff __ Gui - on.

Cui lai - rai ge mes __   a - mors, a - mi - e, s'a __ vos __ non?
Ah! to whom shall I __   give love, My dear, if not __ to __ you?

6. Rondeau. Anonymous, transcribed by Gennrich. This rondeau has a longer text than the preceding one, and it both begins and ends with the refrain. The soloist inserts his comments on the proposition stated in the refrain.

Refrain { A *Ainssi doit on aler*   *Thus should one go*
          B   *a son ami,*   *To one's lover,*
          a   bon fait [a] de-   [For] it is good to enjoy oneself.
              porter.
Refrain   A *Ainssi doit on aler,*   *Thus should one go*
          a   baisier et acoler,   To kiss and embrace,
          b   pour voir le di.   For I hold it to be a truth.
Refrain { A *Ainssi doit on aler*   *Thus should one go*
          B   *a son ami.*   *To one's lover.*

No. 6

Ains - si doit __ on - a - ler __ a son - a - mi, __ bon fait a __ de - por -
O thus, O __ thus should one __ Go to __ one's love, __ For good it __ is __ to

ter. __ Ains - si doit __ on - a - ler, __ bai - sier et __ a - co - ler, __ pour
go. __ O thus, O __ thus __ to go, __ To kiss, to __ kiss __ and love, __ I

voir __ le di. __ Ains - si doit __ on __ a - ler __ a son - a - mi. __
hold __ it true. __ O thus, O __ thus __ should one __ go to __ one's love. __

7. Rondeau. Willamme d' Amiens paignour (William of Amiens, pagan), transcribed by Gennrich. Here is a rondeau of substantial length,* the refrain alone having three lines. In principle, however, it is like the simpler example given above (No. 6).

Refrain {
  A *Amours me maint u cuer,*   *Love dwells in my heart.*
  B *ki me fait languir,*   *It makes me languish*
  C *se ne me veut werpir,*   *And will not leave me.*

  a *el ne m'est mie suer,*   It is no friend of mine.

Refrain A *Amours me maint u cuer,*   Love dwells in my heart,

  a *ains m'a fait geter puer*   But makes me drive out

  b *le sage desir*   The wise desire

  c *qui me dëust garir.*   Which might cure me.

Refrain {
  A *Amours me maint u cuer,*   Love dwells in my heart.
  B *ki me fait languir,*   *It makes me languish*
  C *se ne me veut werpir.*   *And will not leave me.*

No. 7

* The actual length of these pieces, of course, depends on the number of verses. In all these examples only the first verse is given.

puer   le   sa - ge____   de -   sir qui   me   dé -
out   Wise de - sire,____   de -   sire Which might be

ust____   ga - rir.   A - mours me____ maint u____ cuer,
cur -   ing__ me.   Ah! Love dwells__ in   my____ heart.

ki   me fait____ lan -   guir, se   ne   me veut____ wer - pir.
Ah!   it makes__   me____   sad, And will not let____ me__ be.

CHAPTER

❦ 14 ❦

Major and Minor Keys: Background and Terminology

The scale system of standard modern practice really consists of only two "modes"—one of them like the major scale on C or F, and the other like the minor scale on D or *a*. The special feature of the system is that these two kinds of scales are constructed not merely on a few tones, but on each of the twelve chromatic steps. This gives a complete system of twenty-four scales—twelve of them major, and twelve of them minor. Before we describe the standard modern system in detail, let us discuss briefly some of the events in scale development between the time of the chant modes and the time the newer system became established.

FROM MODES TO KEYS

Scale systems, of course, are formed in response to the demands of music itself. The early modal system was formed to support a kind of music which consisted only of unaccompanied vocal melody, and it did this extremely well, because it offered a great variety of step patterns and a sensitive regulation of ranges and points of tonal emphasis. Our modern system has less to offer to a purely melodic style than had the old church modes. But the modes designed for chant were no sooner well formulated than they began to have to meet the demands of a development which was to distinguish Western music from that of other cultures—*polyphony* (Greek: *polys*, many; *phonos*, sound).

Polyphony results when two or more melodic lines are sounded simultaneously. This complex art grew gradually from one-line chant melody, first by the addition of parallel moving melodic lines, and then by the addition of lines moving in contrary directions to the original chant.

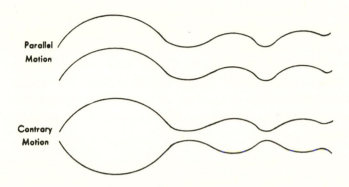

Parallel
Motion

Contrary
Motion

The art of polyphony, after passing through many stages of technical development, eventually enabled composers to write as many as four or more quite independent melodic lines which, nevertheless, blended smoothly into harmonious sounds. But it can easily be seen that the modes in their original sense were destroyed by the development of polyphonic writing. The listener could no longer focus his attention on the variety of step patterns in a melodic line when there were several of them going on at the same time. Also, the ranges of the single lines lost their individual meanings, because the senses for high and low and the feeling for the relations of the tones to the final were captivated by the more striking features of the whole texture, particularly the harmonies that were formed. Although it was possible to analyze the modal qualities of each of the single lines which formed the polyphony (and this was actually done by theorists), such an analysis was more or less irrelevant, as the main effect of the music resulted from the sound of the whole, not the separate parts. Aside from these matters of texture, which made the modal elements difficult to perceive, the scale forms themselves were altered by accidentals which were used to avoid tritones and supply leading tones in endings. And yet, in spite of these many features which were against the nature of the old church modes, some thread of connection with them was always maintained, perhaps because Gregorian melodies were incorporated within so much polyphonic music.

In the sixteenth century, the modal system was expanded to include the two remaining useful diatonic finals—*a* and *c*. The expansion of the system was the work of Heinrich Glarean (Glareanus), a Swiss humanist and theorist, who in 1547 published a book called *Dodecachordon* ("harp of twelve strings") because in it he discussed increasing the number of the modes from eight to twelve. These modes were identified by Greek names rather than by numbers, following a practice which had been instituted earlier. Since all references to modes in later music or in musical writings use these names,* we shall list them here. The sixteenth-century modes were as follows:

	AUTHENTIC				PLAGAL	
	Final	*Range*			*Final*	*Range*
Dorian	D	D-d	Hypodorian		D	A-a
Phrygian	E	E-e	Hypophrygian		E	B-b
Lydian	F	F-f	Hypolydian		F	C-c
Mixolydian	G	G-g	Hypomixolydian		G	D-d
Aeolian	a	a-aa	Hypoaeolian		a	E-e
Ionian	c	c-cc	Hypoionian		c	G-g

Only a little more than fifty years after the publication of the *Dodecachordon*, certain Italian composers who were no longer content with the existing styles (Monteverdi, in particular) laid the foundations for a new style that depended very little on polyphony. These composers were especially interested in opera, which was a brand-new form, and they felt that many-voiced music obscured the all-important text. A few accompanying chords properly placed, on the other hand, were capable of high dramatic effect without obscuring the text, or drawing too much of the listener's attention from the words. What resulted, in a technical sense, from the experiments of these composers and their reduction of the importance of polyphony in their dramatic compositions was a new method of construction which was essentially the one we learn today in the kind of study called *harmony*.

* For example, the third movement of Beethoven's String Quartet, Opus 132, "in the Lydian mode." Also, collectors such as Cecil Sharp apply these names to diatonic folk-melodies. References to modes in other modern writings on music use the names as given here, but it may be pointed out that in ancient Greek writings (such as Plato's *Republic*) the names refer to entirely different scales.

The older method of construction used in polyphony was called *counterpoint* (Latin: *punctus contra punctum*, note against note); according to this method the musical texture was built up by the addition of individual melodic lines, one to the other. According to the newer method, *chords,** which had previously *resulted* from the adding together of melodies, were regarded as prearranged and fixed units, and the method of construction shifted from the adding together of single lines (counterpoint) to the individual placement and cementing together of the chord blocks (harmony). More than a century after its inception in the works of the early baroque Italian composers, this method was formulated in a definitive way by the French composer J. P. Rameau, in his *Traité de l'harmonie* (1722). Since that time every book on the kind of harmony we understand as "traditional" has been heavily indebted to Rameau's remarkable treatise.

It was only natural that the new harmonic style should soon find the polyphonically adapted modes of the sixteenth century to be an inadequate supply of tonal material. Actually this system did not possess as great a variety as the number of modes implied. The use of accidentals and the difficulty of perceiving plagal forms of the modes in a polyphonic texture reduced the effective number of scales to considerably less than twelve, all of them conforming either to the major or the minor scale patterns. And when the "*nuove musiche*" appeared, lacking the old polyphonic elaboration, the urge must have been intensified for a greater variety of starting points for the major- and minor-type scales. New tonal environments, as well as the possibility of more rapid changes of environment, were needed to make up for the loss of contrapuntal density in the new style. But before it was to become possible to start a major or minor scale on any tones except the few finals of the modes, or to change finals rapidly within a single piece, the science of keyboard tuning had to solve certain acoustical problems. The solution of these problems was imperative also because one of the features of the "new music" was, after centuries of vocal domination, the emergence of purely instrumental and instrumentally accompanied vocal music as major fields of expression.

* Two or more notes may receive the general designation "harmony"; an interval is a harmony. But a "chord" is at least three notes.

EQUAL TEMPERAMENT: KEYBOARD TUNING

The first necessary condition to permit the construction of major and minor scales on any of the twelve tones within the octave was a keyboard tuned in perfect symmetry. All half-steps had to be exactly one twelfth and all whole-steps one sixth of an octave so that the scales would have the same intonation, regardless of the starting point. It is obvious that if some half-steps were more and others were less than one twelfth of an octave, a different intonation would result from each starting point, depending on where the too small or too large intervals happened to fall. And yet, nature tricked the earliest keyboard tuners into just that sort of asymmetrical tuning.

Nature's trick was that she made it impossible for keyboard tuners to rely on what would have seemed to be the most obvious source for correct intonation—the well-known sounds of the simplest intervals, such as fifths, fourths, and major thirds. From the beginning tuners had to face the fact (known since ancient times from mathematical calculations) that adding together series of these pure intervals would result in an eventual disagreement in pitch between the starting tones and the last tones to be derived. To draw an analogy, it is as though inches and feet were fixed sizes in nature, but twelve inches when added together exceeded or fell short of a foot. The inches would have to be altered to fit correctly into any yardstick constructed in even feet. Likewise, in tuning keyboards, all smaller intervals have to be altered to fit correctly into pure octaves.

If, in tuning a keyboard, we were to start at the bottom and tune upward in perfect fifths, we would discover that the duplication of the starting note seven octaves higher would be out of tune (too high). We can best demonstrate this phenomenon, which was of such serious consequence to practical music, by means of figures. And to do this we need to make use of a system of tonal measurement introduced by the English theorist, A. J. Ellis (1814–90). In Ellis's system the octave is divided into 1,200 parts called *cents*.* Accord-

---

* In Appendix II a chart is given which shows in cents the natural sizes of the intervals in the overtone series, as well as the artificial sizes needed for keyboard tuning. See page 211.

ing to this method of measurement, a fifth in its natural intonation has the size of approximately 702 cents.

Here is this problem shown in figures:

Superimposition of 12 fifths, beginning with, and returning to A:

$$\begin{array}{cccccc} 1 & 2 & 3 & 4 & 5 & 6 \\ \text{a-e,} & \text{e-b,} & \text{b-f}\sharp, & \text{f}\sharp\text{-c}\sharp, & \text{c}\sharp\text{-g}\sharp, & \text{g}\sharp\text{-d}\sharp, \end{array}$$

$$\begin{array}{cccccc} 7 & 8 & 9 & 10 & 11 & 12 \\ \text{d}\sharp\text{-a}\sharp, & \text{a}\sharp\text{-e}\sharp, & \text{e}\sharp\text{-b}\sharp, & \text{c}\natural(\text{b}\sharp)\text{-g}\natural, & \text{g-d,} & \text{d-a} \end{array}$$

$$12 \times 702 = 8424$$

Superimposition of 7 octaves:

$$7 \times 1200 = 8400$$

The discrepancy:
$$\begin{array}{l} 8424 \ \ (12 \ \text{fifths}) \\ \underline{-8400 \ \ \ (7 \ \text{octaves})} \\ 24 \ \text{cents} \end{array}$$

This discrepancy, present in theory and in fact, but almost impossible actually to hear with the distance of seven octaves between the two A's, could be observed easily if we followed the kind of practical procedure actually used by tuners: adjusting a single octave in the middle of the keyboard first, and then tuning the rest of the keyboard with these tones as a "bearing." In forming a bearing, each newly derived tone is dropped downward into its place within a single octave.

The discrepancy of twenty-four cents which would show up between the low and high A's of the model octave is entirely within our capacity to distinguish, as we can detect as little as three cents' difference between tones in the middle range of the keyboard, sounding at moderate loudness. This tiny interval of twenty-four cents is called the *Pythagorean comma*, because it was supposed to have been observed first by the ancient Greek mathematician, astronomer, and music theorist, Pythagoras (*c.* 550 B.C.).

The problem of keyboard tuning utilizing fifths has always been how to absorb the Pythagorean comma by dividing it into imperceptible deviations among the twelve tones of the chromatic scale. The earliest reasonably successful solution was the *mean-tone system*, developed around the beginning of the sixteenth century. This system used a fifth of 697 instead of 702 cents, and was a practical method for music still attached to the modes. But it exposed other errors of pitch which prevented the further development of the scale system.

A clear proposal for tuning keyboards in half-steps of equal size, or *equal temperament*, using fifths of 700 cents, a deviation from the natural size too small to be disturbing, was made by the French mathematician and theorist Mersenne in 1635. This was just the right time for Mersenne's proposal to appear, as the need was plain for the expansion of the scale system, and for the correction of the falseness of keyboard instruments whenever the music tried to venture too far from the white keys. But the practical adoption of equal temperament came about very slowly, extending through the seventeenth and eighteenth centuries, and even into the nineteenth. The most famous celebration of its advantages was Bach's *Well-Tempered Keyboard*, which consisted of two volumes, each containing twenty-four preludes and fugues written within major and minor scales on all of the twelve tones of the octave.

TERMINOLOGY (1): KEYS, THE NEW MEANING OF "MODE"

Once the major scale on C, the *"modus lascivus"* of the Middle Ages, had found its way into the modal system, it began gradually to assume a place of prominence. Modern harmonic feeling recognized the major form of the scale as tonally superior and more stable than the minor form, and the old listing which began the system with the scale on D (Dorian mode) finally gave way in the seventeenth century to a new listing beginning with C. The choice of the C major scale as a starting point rather than F or G was natural, since C requires no accidentals.

Along with the choice of C as the principal major scale, A became the principal minor scale, because although every minor scale requires accidentals in ascending, this scale was the only one which needed no accidentals for its descending form.

Before showing how the whole standard modern scale system is erected on these two starting points, we need first to establish certain terminologies.

The scales of the modern system outline the tones of *keys*, not modes. The word "mode" remains in use, but only to define the major or minor quality of a scale or key. The C major and all other major scales are said to be in the *major mode*, while the A minor and all other minor scales are said to be in the *minor mode*.

In the last few paragraphs we have used the neutral designation of capital letters for scales and keys. But in correct modern theoretical usage it is customary when referring to keys or scales by letter to use *capital letters for major*, and *small letters for minor* (e.g., C major, *a* minor). When a key or scale is mentioned from here on, the letter form will indicate major or minor mode, not, as it has up to now, a specific pitch in the gamut.

TERMINOLOGY (2): PITCH DESIGNATIONS

When a specific pitch has to be identified by letter, a newer system will be used, which covers the whole range of the keyboard. This system, for the middle of the keyboard, is as follows:

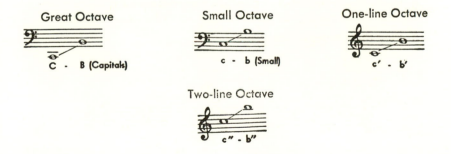

For higher octaves, additional vertical lines are added to the upper right of the letter (Three-line Octave, Four-line Octave, etc.).

The sign 8 ----- is sometimes employed when the tones of the extreme high register are used. This sign means that the tones under the broken line are to be played an octave higher than they are written. Since the treble clef is the highest one available, the use of the *ottava* (Italian: octave) sign for very high passages may save labor in writing many ledger lines, and may make a melody in the extreme high register more readable.

The reverse of the octave sign given above is the indication 8---------- (*ottava bassa*), which may be placed below the tones in the bass clef to indicate that they are to sound an octave lower than they are written.

After either of the octave signs, the word *loco* (Italian: place) means to return to the original octave.

Here are the tones of the lowest region of the keyboard, shown by the use of the *ottava bassa* sign. The terminology "one-line," "two-line," etc., is not used here, but vertical lines are placed to the lower left of the letter names.

EXPERIMENT 49.

a. Write under the tones of the following example the correct letter symbols, showing the exact octaves in which they occur.

b. Play these tones on the piano.

MAJOR KEYS, THE CIRCLE OF FIFTHS, KEY SIGNATURES

If the scale on C (which requires no accidentals) is to be our model and starting point, let us see what accidentals will be involved when we try to produce this pattern beginning on other tones.

We know already from the altered modes that the scales on F with b♭ and G with f♯ are major-type scales. The relationships of these two keys to the starting point C will provide us with the clue to the arrangement of the whole system.

EXPERIMENT 50.

Referring to the diagram below, answer the following questions:
a. What is the interval relationship between C and G? Between C and F?

b. What step in the scale on G requires a sharp? What step in F requires a flat?

It will be observed in the above experiment that the key with one sharp (G) is a fifth above C, and the key with one flat (F) is a fourth above (or, as it is sometimes counted, a fifth below). Also, that the sharp is added on the seventh step of G, and the flat on the fourth step of F. The names and accidentals, in order, of the other keys may be deduced by carrying this relationship forward through successive stages. Whatever the starting point:

1. The next key using sharps will be a fifth above. It will retain the existing sharps, and add a new one on the seventh step.

2. The next key using flats will be a fourth above (or fifth below). It will retain the existing flats, and add a new one on the fourth step.

EXPERIMENT 51.

a. On what tone does the key with two sharps occur? Two flats?

b. On what note is the second sharp? The second flat?

The whole system of major keys in sharps and flats may be shown in a diagram called the *circle of fifths*. The sharp keys are arranged in clockwise order on the right-hand side of the circle. The flat keys are arranged on the left side in counterclockwise order. At six accidentals the sharps and flats overlap (which would not be possible without equal temperament). The keys with six sharps and six flats are enharmonically equivalent.

The accidentals in keys are placed at the start of the piece, immediately after the clef, and before the time signature. They are referred to as *key signatures*.

F Major   G Major

The accidentals in the key signature affect the tones in all octaves —not only the ones on which the accidentals happen to be placed. Accidentals *not* in the signature continue to affect only the tones to which they are applied.

The correct form for indicating the accidentals on the staff must be memorized, since it follows no rule other than convention.

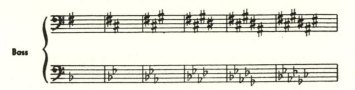

EXPERIMENT 52.

Fill in the remainder of this diagram, continuing in the same manner as it begins.

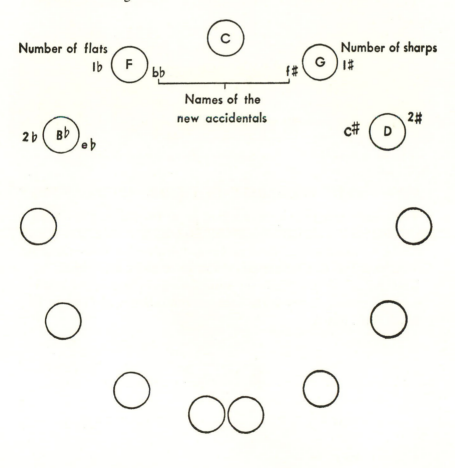

EXPERIMENT 53.

a. Write out all twelve major scales, with key signatures, through one octave (ascending only) in treble clef. Do the same in bass clef. Choose starting points which are least likely to require the use of ledger lines.

b. Play through all these scales at the piano until even the most complicated keys become familiar.

The six sharps and flats are arranged in the alto and tenor clefs as follows:

MINOR KEYS, THE CIRCLE OF FIFTHS, ACCIDENTALS

The minor scale on *a* is the starting point for the circle of minor keys. Since this scale has no accidentals in its signature, it is paired with the C major scale. Minor and major scales that share the same signatures in this manner are called *relative* majors and minors.

The clue to the relative major and minor coupling is: the relative minor of any major key is the same as the relation of C to *a*—i.e., a minor third down.

EXPERIMENT 54.

Name the relative minors of the following major keys:
B♭ A B D♭ F D

EXPERIMENT 55.

Fill in the remainder of this diagram of the circle of fifths for minor keys, continuing in the same manner as it begins.

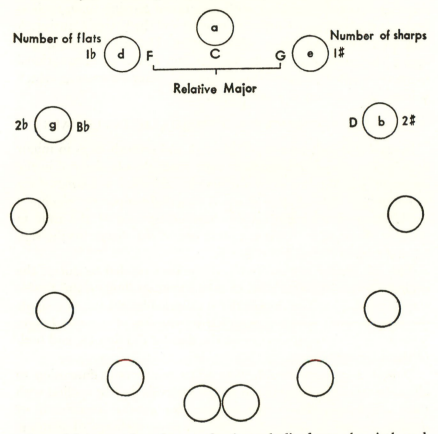

In writing out the minor scales in melodic form, the sixth and seventh steps must be raised in ascending and lowered in descending, just as they were in the secular scales on D and *a. These accidentals are never placed in the signature.* Here is an example (c minor, relative minor of Eb major):

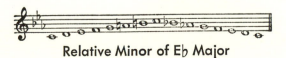

Relative Minor of Eb Major

The sixth and seventh steps are raised in this instance by canceling the flats in the signature. They are lowered in descending by restoring the flats.

It may be perceived that another type of major-minor relationship can exist between keys with a common starting tone, such as between the scale given above (c minor) and the key of C major. A relationship of this kind is called *parallel*. The parallel major and minor association is of somewhat less importance in conventional harmonic usage than the relative major and minor association, which is based on common key signatures.

DOUBLE ACCIDENTALS: CHROMATIC INTERVALS

In making the alterations of the sixth and seventh steps in minor keys, it is sometimes necessary to raise tones already sharped in the signature. For this we need the accidental called a *double sharp* (symbol: ✕). The double sharp is canceled simply by placing a single sharp or a natural on the next occurrence of the tone in question. Some older editions cancel one of the sharps by the sign ♮♯, and both of them by the sign ♮♮.

The companion to the double sharp (not needed to notate the ordinary scales, but often used in enharmonic spelling) is the *double flat* (symbol: ♭♭). The double flat is canceled by the use of a single flat sign, or both flats are canceled by the use of a natural sign. Some older editions cancel one of the flats by the sign ♮♭, and both of them by the sign ♮♮.

Double sharps and double flats add a whole new dimension to chromatic spelling. While even simple intervals may be spelled with these accidentals, they often account for *doubly diminished* or *doubly augmented* intervals. Here are some spellings of diatonic and chromatic intervals, many of which involve double sharps and double flats:

EXPERIMENT 56.

a. Write the correct names of the intervals given above.

b. Play these intervals on the piano.

c. Write a simpler enharmonic spelling for each interval on the blank staves.

The student may well ask what possible purpose could be served by these complicated spellings. The answer, as far as intervals themselves are concerned, is that they serve no purpose. But later on, in the study of harmony, such formations may sometimes be unavoidable. For this reason, fluency in reading difficult spellings is a prerequisite to the study of harmony.

EXPERIMENT 57.

a. Write out all twelve minor scales, with key signatures, making the necessary alterations to produce the melodic form. Write the scales through one octave, ascending and descending, in treble clef. Do the same in bass clef. Choose starting points which are least likely to require the use of ledger lines.

b. Play through all these scales at the piano until even the most complicated keys become familiar.

VARIOUS FORMS OF THE MINOR SCALE

Besides the melodic minor, traditional theory acknowledges two other forms of the minor scale: the *natural minor*, and the *harmonic minor*.

The natural minor is simply the modal form of the scale, with low sixth and seventh steps.

Natural Minor Scale

This scale has little use in harmonic practice, and after it is given in the opening chapters of harmony books as the "original form of the minor scale from which the others were derived," nothing much more is said about it. Nothing needs to be said, either, as it is really a mode, and lacks a leading tone, which is an element of the utmost importance in harmony.

The harmonic minor scale has the raised leading tone, but the sixth step remains in its low form. The scale is the same whether ascending or descending.

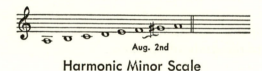

Aug. 2nd

Harmonic Minor Scale

The low sixth and high seventh steps form an augmented second, which is a symptom of the chromatic formula contained in the upper region of this scale:

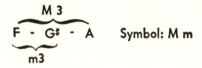

Because of this chromaticism, the harmonic minor scale is ordinarily not used for melody. In fact, traditional harmony in its simpler forms forbids carrying a melodic line across the gap between its sixth and seventh steps. Since we have seen that scales are originally a derivation from melody, we may ask how it happens that there is such a scale as this one which is not entirely fit for melodic use.

The harmonic minor scale is aptly named, as it consists of the tones in the commonest harmonies (chords) of the minor mode. These harmonies contain the low sixth and high seventh steps; therefore, the scale shows these tones, ignoring their melodic awkwardness. For harmonic purposes (e.g., chord construction) the harmonic form of the scale is generally used, and for melodic purposes (the lines which move above the harmonies) the melodic form is favored. One of the difficulties of writing harmony in the minor mode is to use these forms of the scale appropriately, and to keep them out of chromatic conflict with each other.

⚜ 15 ⚜

Major and Minor Keys: Melody-Writing Without Text, as though for Instruments

We can develop a thorough familiarity with the system of major and minor keys, and synthesize a number of our previously acquired skills, by turning now to a kind of melody-writing not directed toward any specific historical style. This approach would be the "abstract" one, as opposed to the "stylistic" approach employed in the chapters on chant and French medieval secular melody (see the previous discussion of the approaches to compositional techniques, pages 115–117).

One may ask why this sort of approach is adopted in dealing with the scale material of the most familiar styles. Couldn't the stylistic approach be used to even greater advantage here than before, since its models would be the most familiar ones available?

THE IMPORTANCE OF HARMONY IN TRADITIONAL MELODY

The reason we cannot at this stage compose melodies in familiar style (except, if we wish, "by ear") is that the principal means of regulating them lies within the sphere of harmony, and harmony is a whole new subject which in itself requires an effort at least comparable to that exerted so far in the present study. Only after a fairly substantial acquaintance with harmony could we attempt stylistically controlled experiments in melody-writing along traditional lines.

Melody, as we have observed it here, is one of the basic elements of music, more primitive in a way and yet more subtle than harmony, which is a late and sophisticated development, characteristic, in fact, only of Western culture. And yet in the period of our classical and romantic music (roughly 1750–1900) the newcomer, harmony, succeeds in dominating its older relative, melody. Many of the most famous melodies of that period show clearly their dependence on underlying harmonies. Each of the well-known examples shown below (and there are many others similar to these) is based on the three tones of one simple chord.

Haydn: Symphony No. 97 in C Major ("Salomon"), bar 14, first movement.

Beethoven: Symphony No. 3 in E♭ Major ("Eroica"), bar 3, first movement.

Brahms: Violin Concerto in D Major, beginning of the first movement.

These melodies, while less free-flowing than the lines of Gregorian chant or old folk-tunes, function superbly in their proper settings —that is, in large forms which rely extensively on the constructive and expressive power of harmony.

EXPERIMENT 58.

a. Try to think of other themes from standard literature which illustrate this type of construction.

b. Sing themes of this type extemporaneously.

In melodies of this period which do not progress so obviously along the lines of chords, the influence of harmony shows itself in other ways. In an otherwise diatonic melody accidentals may occur which can really be explained only in terms of the underlying harmony. The opening of the second movement of Beethoven's Fifth Symphony, for example, has A's and E's, although it is in the key of A♭ major. This is not a manifestation of chromatic melodic construction; these tones enter the melody through the influence of harmony.

MAJOR AND MINOR MELODIES: PROCEDURE (FORM AND RHYTHM), NOTATION

The above examples should have provided a glimpse of the importance of harmony to the composition of melodies in the styles of the late eighteenth and nineteenth centuries. This fact, however, need not prevent us at this point from writing melodies which make use of the major and minor scales. We can set up our own conditions and procedures, which will give us the experience of using the scale material at hand, whether or not the results closely resemble the styles of any particular composers. And we can thereby close the present study with a synthesis of a number of our previously acquired skills.

We shall compose small pieces without text in a style more appropriate to instruments than to voices. As the first stage in writing these melodies, we shall repeat (on an enlarged scale) the procedures of Chapter 8 in composing rhythmic outlines. The technique applied there to the composition of phrases will be combined here with the technique of making forms, such as those employed in the chants and secular melodies. The procedure for sketching the rhythmical and formal aspects of the pieces will be as follows:

1. Decide first the essential character of the piece. Will it be fast, slow, gay, sad, flowing, heavy? This decision will naturally affect all else that follows.

2. Decide on the broad aspects of the form. Will it be a comparatively unsegmented form, perhaps held together by the repetition of small motives (as in some chants); will it have one of the clearly segmented designs which can be diagrammed by letters (as with the French secular songs); or will it combine these two types?

A deliberate decision of this kind at the beginning is useful in the same way that an architect's ground plan is useful. Even if there are reasons to change or elaborate the plan at later stages, the early planning will not be wasted, as it helps to crystallize one's thoughts.

3. Sketch the rhythm of the pieces above the staff, as with the secular melodies.

The separation of the rhythmic and melodic impulses, of course, is not always necessary, but in the early stages of writing it may help greatly to span the musical time. Having to decide both the rhythmic and melodic aspects at once might be so slow a process as to extinguish the feeling for whole phrases. In writing words, one has to keep pen and mind moving along at a certain pace or the ideas may be lost before the sentences are formed. Likewise, in writing music the rhythmic feeling must push ahead fast enough (no matter what tones are employed) to span full ideas. Once the framework of a formal unit (phrase, or larger section) has been established, the exact tones can be fitted in and polished slowly without the danger of losing the basic idea. Finally, as greater fluency is achieved, the rhythmic and melodic (later on, even harmonic) impulses may be pursued and captured almost simultaneously.

The forms of some of these pieces may involve repetitions of whole sections. There are abbreviations for certain kinds of repetitions which save the labor of writing them out in full. The signs employed for them are:

1. *The Repetition Sign.* The sign :‖ means to repeat the section just completed (a). If this is not the first section of the piece, any other point at which the repetition begins must be set off by the reverse sign ‖: (b). Repetition signs may serve as bar-lines, but they may also be placed at any other point in the measure (c). The diagrams below show the course of the music. The sections above the wavy part of the line are played.

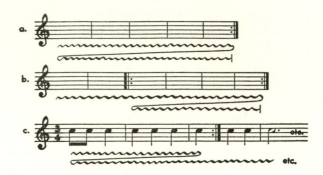

2. *First and Second Endings.* If a repetition is literal except for the very end, the two different endings may be written under brackets: ⌐1. ⌐2. . After the first ending, the repetition takes place, omitting the bars under ⌐1. and proceeding to those under ⌐2. .

3. *D.C. al fine.* This Italian marking, Da capo al fine, "from the head to the end," means to return to the beginning and proceed from there to the point marked "Fine."

4. *D.S. al fine.* Dal segno al fine, "to the sign, and to the end." If the repetition does not go all the way back to the beginning, the point at which it starts is marked by a sign, ⊕ or 𝄋 .

5. *D.C. al segno*. This means "to the beginning until the sign." This indication is used when a special ending is desired after the D.C. At the sign, the D.C. jumps to the remaining part of the piece.

If it is desired to pause a little before making a D.C., or to prolong any tone or rest for the sake of emphasis or clear punctuation, the sign ⌢, called a *corona*, indicates a *fermata* or "hold." During a fermata the flow of the meter is temporarily halted. The sign is placed above the note it affects.

MELODIC MOTION, TONAL ORGANIZATION

When the rhythmic and formal outline has been completed, the tones should be added on the staff below. Here are guides to appropriate melodic conduct in these pieces:

1. The tonal material is, of course, the major and minor scales in all keys.
2. The pieces may be written either in a generalized instrumental style, or for specific instruments.

In the first case, use any one of the four commonest clefs. The exact instrument need not be specified, as various instruments can play treble melodies, others can play alto or tenor melodies, and still others can play bass melodies. The ranges for melodies written in the generalized instrumental style should be approximately the tones on the staff within the chosen clefs.

In the second case, the ranges should be those of specific instruments, and the notations and styles should be idiomatic. A previous playing knowledge of the instrument would be the best reason to choose to write this sort of melody. However, there is a discussion in Appendix II which gives the ranges and notational peculiarities of the various orchestral instruments. If desired, the present project may be elevated into a lesson in instrumentation as well as melody-writing by coordinating it with the material of Appendix II.

3. The treatment of leaps will be freer than in the melodies previously composed. If the piece is in a generalized instrumental style, an occasional leap of a seventh, ninth, or tenth may be introduced. If the piece is written for a specific instrument, leaps of more than a tenth may be used when they are particularly idiomatic (e.g., the clarinet easily makes leaps of a twelfth).

4. The tritone, regardless of the instrumental style that is used, calls for special attention in well-regulated diatonic melodies. With modern scales there is no longer any reason to avoid tritone leaps, but they should be handled with some regard for the leading tone contained in them. This leading tone should usually follow its natural inclination and progress to the principal note of the scale, which we now call, rather than "final," the *tonic*. For example:

In the above examples, the tritone leap is *to* the leading tone, which then *resolves* to the tonic. If the progression is reversed, the other tone (although it is not a leading tone) should also move by half-step progression. For example:

To summarize: *after a tritone leap, a half-step progression is desirable.*

The ear, after experiencing the insecurity of a tritone progression, is comforted by the closeness and ease of half-step progressions; through conditioning, perhaps, we even expect these progressions after we hear tritones. Almost the same degree of satisfaction is experienced even when a few other tones intervene before the expected resolution takes place. For example:

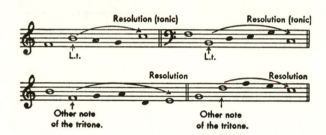

The tritone is exposed in the barest manner when neither of the expected tones ever arrives, as in the following examples:

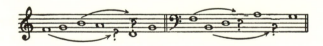

Groups of tones such as those in the above example ought to be avoided in a smoothly regulated diatonic melody, especially cases like the first one, in which the highest point of the melodic line is the leading tone. This tone, when exposed at the top of a melodic curve, remains easily in the memory; and if it is not canceled by the appearance immediately or shortly afterward of the tonic note, a feeling of irresolution and incompleteness may result.

5. Use the melodic minor scale, and treat the sixth and seventh steps sensitively, observing their upward and downward tendencies in the line, and using the ascending and descending forms of the scale accordingly.

As for the tritones and the chromatic intervals and groupings in the minor mode, continue generally to avoid them, as in the secular songs. But on those occasions when their use seems desirable, the leading tone contained in them should be handled as in the tritone of the major mode; the leading tone should be resolved immediately, or shortly afterward. For example:

The augmented second between the sixth and seventh steps, as in the harmonic minor, should not be used, even though the leading tone is satisfactorily resolved in the ascending progression. For this situation, use the much smoother melodic form of the scale:

6. The tonal organization, such as can be effected without harmony, should be very much the same as in the previous melodic projects.

Pieces may begin on any tone of the scale.

Pieces should end on the tonic.

Phrase endings may be closed (on the tonic), or open (on some tone other than the tonic, giving the impression that the music is still to continue).

Open endings should occur most often on the fifth step of

the scale, called the *dominant*. This is the term which is familiar to us from chant melodies, and its function here is not unlike its earlier one, as a sort of opposite pole to the "final" or tonic. Through the influence of harmony, however, the dominant has an even more powerful significance in the major and minor key system than its early equivalent had in the modes.

EXPERIMENT 59.

Compose melodies in major and minor keys, as though for instruments, according to the procedures outlined above.

CONCLUSION

After the experience derived from the composition of melodies in the major and minor keys, we reach a turning point in our studies; the next stage must involve writing two or more melodies together (counterpoint), or placing chords together with melodies (harmony). These two subjects, counterpoint and harmony, form the central part of the composer's technical training, and a knowledge of them is also indispensable for an intelligent approach to the problems of performance. We are ready, after the preparations made here, to begin the study of harmony according to any standard method. As for the subject of counterpoint, however, the situation is a little more complex.

Counterpoint is taught on the basis of two distinct historical styles: that of the sixteenth century (Palestrina, Orlando di Lasso); and that of the eighteenth century (Bach). These styles are fundamentally different, and while we would be able to start the first one at this point, the second will have to wait until after we have completed the study of harmony.

Counterpoint in the sixteenth-century style conforms to the essential nature of polyphony as it has been described above: its method is to begin with a single melodic line and to add other lines, producing harmonies which are of a prescribed kind, to be sure, but which are, nevertheless, the product of the melodic lines. The preparation afforded by the writing of modal melodies is ideal for the study of sixteenth-century counterpoint, and a smooth line of technical progress may be achieved by following this text immediately with some sort of sixteenth-century counterpoint, before the study of harmony. Later on, the study of harmony itself could not fail to benefit from this sequence, as one of its major problems is the polyphonic aspect of the lines which are formed in the various parts when the chord blocks are placed next to each other. This important interrelation of the contrapuntal and harmonic elements may, perhaps, be clarified by the following diagram:

These lines (1, 2, 3), added together by the contrapuntal process, produce harmonies (a, b, c, etc.):

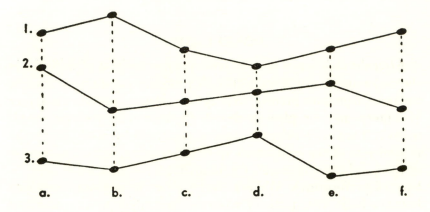

These chords (1, 2, 3, etc.), added successively by the harmonic process, produce lines (a, b, c):

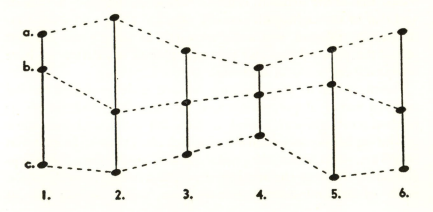

Unlike sixteenth-century counterpoint, that used in the eight-eenth century can be considered only after the study of harmony, as its method involves the decoration and elaboration of an under-lying chord structure into a dense linear texture. Bach, for instance, preferred to teach his students four-part harmony before he al-lowed them to write counterpoint, even in two parts. According to his point of view, the melodic lines could not be allowed to form harmonies on their own terms; they had to express or imply chord movements of the same kind as those present in the plainly harmonic pieces of the period, such as *chorales* (hymns).

For our own studies, then, we may proceed next either to the counterpoint of the sixteenth century, or to traditional harmony. The preceding chapters, especially the last two, are a good founda-tion for the study of harmony; and for that matter, the emphasis throughout Part II on melodic lines will serve us in very good stead also, since no chord progressions can be entirely convincing without smoothness of melodic treatment in the various parts.

If the above suggestions point out the future courses for the aspects of theory which deal with writing music, how about the con-tinuation of the skills in performance and perception developed in Part I?

There are many texts which deal with the performance and per-ception of rhythms, and with sight-singing. Any one of them which offers a sufficient challenge to the skills already acquired will be helpful. On the other hand, once the first hurdles have been over-come, perhaps the best means of developing performance skills from there on is simply to perform—either on an instrument, by singing, or still better, by a balanced mixture of these two fundamental kinds of music-making. Then, many problems (especially of reading) which had to be solved at first in a conscious and deliberate way will, as the performer acquires experience, become second nature, and cease to be problems at all. Reading in the musical language may then approach the degree of fluency we are all expected to possess in the reading of words.

One can easily see that a clear and definite conclusion for a study such as we have attempted here is virtually impossible to establish; every one of the phases of music theory introduced in this text has a necessary continuation. And still, the limits of an introductory study ought to be defined at some point. If we must define them here, let us do so with the hope that the student's interest will have been stimulated sufficiently to send him onward to the advanced continuations of these studies.

✠1✠

Notes on the Physics of Music

In Chapter 1, terms such as "tone" and "pitch" were used without definition; it was assumed, no doubt rightfully, that everyone has some conception of the meaning of these words. The real definitions of these terms, and certain others, necessarily involve physics, and at that stage such definitions would have led us away from the more important business of learning about the basic sounds (intervals) by means of our voices and ears. Now, however, with some actual musical activity behind us, we can go back to the problem of basic definitions on a more scientific plane.

In opening a discussion of the scientific aspects of sound, we face a quite considerable problem of simplification and condensation. Sound, which to a practicing musician is simply what he hears, is an enormously complex phenomenon. A really full investigation would have to include not only the more or less easily observable physics of external sound, but the physiology of the ear, and the mysterious psychology of the mind's reactions to what is relayed to it by the ear. We shall limit ourselves here by omitting all discussions of hearing or psychological effects, and proceed backward from the point at which we come into contact with the sound (at the eardrum) to brief discussions of vibrations, tone and noise, and overtones. Some connection will be established with familiar musical instruments by discussions of vibrating strings, vibrating air columns, and vibrating plates, membranes, and bells.

CHARACTERISTICS OF TONE

Sound, as we experience it, is at first a physiological event; it is a series of alternately high and low air pressures on the eardrum (*tympanum*), a membrane which lies a short distance down the canal leading from the outer visible part of the ear.

One high-pressure and one low-pressure area together make up what is called a *cycle*, or a *vibration*.

The number of cycles per second is the *frequency*, which we perceive as the *pitch* of the sound; the higher the frequency, the higher the pitch.

The difference in air pressure between the high and low phases of the cycle is the *amplitude*, which we perceive as the *volume*, or *loudness;* the greater the pressure difference, the greater the volume.*

The following diagram may help to make clear the meanings of the terms cycle, frequency, and amplitude:

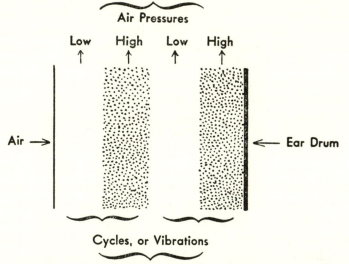

Difference in high and low pressures = amplitude (volume)

Air Pressures

Low   High   Low   High

Air →   ← Ear Drum

Cycles, or Vibrations

Number of cycles per second = frequency (pitch)

Air, the medium which carries the sound from its source to the ear, resembles water in that it may transmit more than one group of cycles (or "waves") at the same time. The whole structure of the sound may consist of large principal waves and smaller subordi-

* This statement is true only in comparing the volumes of two tones of the same pitch. Volume, or loudness to the ear, is determined not only by the amplitude of the tone at its source, but by the variability at different pitch levels of the ear's receptive capacities.

nate waves or ripples. The large waves produce the sound which we call the *fundamental* or *first partial*. The pitch of a tone is determined by the frequency of the fundamental. The smaller waves are called variously partials (*second partial, third partial*, etc.), or *harmonics*, or *overtones*. The partials above the fundamental determine the *timbre* or *tone quality* of the sound. Various instruments and voices are different in tone quality because their various structures emphasize different partials.

We can better understand the nature of a tone with its fundamental and other partials if we examine the behavior of a vibrating string, which is one of the commonest sources of musical tone.

THE VIBRATING STRING

If a string at rest is agitated by plucking or bowing, it moves from its original position to a certain degree of displacement. Its elasticity then causes it to rebound to a position of similar displacement on the opposite side of the point of rest. These movements together constitute a cycle. The frequency with which this cycle occurs, as stated before, will determine the pitch; and the degree of displacement (amplitude) will determine the loudness.

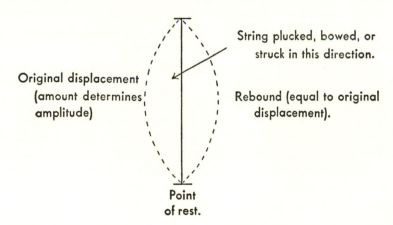

String plucked, bowed, or struck in this direction.

Original displacement (amount determines amplitude)

Rebound (equal to original displacement).

Point of rest.

The vibration of the whole string produces the fundamental sound; at the same time there are secondary vibrations involving subdivisions of the string. These vibrations are of smaller displacement (softer sound) and greater frequency (higher pitch) than the fundamental, and they are the ones which produce the higher partials, or overtones.

The subdivision of the string into partial vibrations occurs according to the series 1, ½, ⅓, ¼, ⅕, etc.; the string vibrates as a whole (1), in two equal parts (½ + ½), in three equal parts (⅓ + ⅓ + ⅓), in four parts, five parts, and so on, divided into smaller and smaller fragments, theoretically to infinity.

The diagram below shows the simultaneous vibration of a string throughout its full length (first partial, or fundamental), and in halves (second partial):

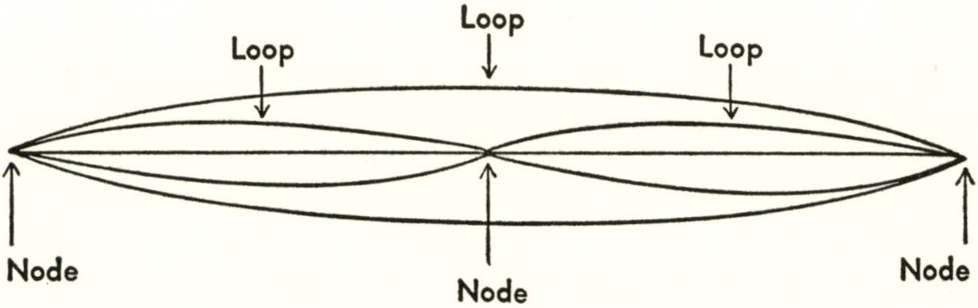

At the ends of the string, and at the points of division, the string is less active. The less active points are called *nodes*. The points of widest vibration are called *antinodes*, or *loops*.

All the sound that we perceive as *tone* has partials conforming to the series given above. A *noise*, therefore, may be defined as a sound with partials of other irregular proportions (e.g., 1, ⅖, 3/7, etc.).*

If all other factors are equal (tension, thickness, weight, etc.) *frequency is inversely proportional to string length*. That is, the shorter the string, the higher the pitch. We can conclude from this rule that the frequency of the first subdivision of a whole string into half lengths (second partial, as in the diagram above) would be twice that of the fundamental. If the fundamental were to have a frequency of 110 cycles, the half sections (each of them) would be vibrating at 220 cycles.

Expressed in musical tones, the above frequencies give the interval of an octave:

* For instance, see the partials of a kettledrum, given on page 216.

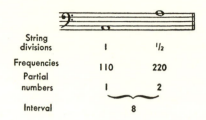

Just as the frequency of the second partial is derived by multiplying the frequency of the fundamental by two, the frequency of the third partial may be found by multiplying by three. Expressed in musical tones, the third partial adds a fifth above the octave formed by the first and second partials:

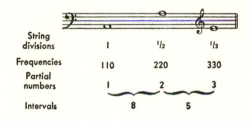

INTERVAL PROPORTIONS, THE PARTIAL SERIES

The frequencies of the octave expressed as proportions would be 110:220, or, in reduced form, 1:2. Those of the fifth would be 220:330, or 2:3. It may be noted that the partial numbers between which the intervals occur state correctly the proportions of their frequencies; if the interval's position in the partial series is known, its proportions may be easily determined without the necessity of reducing large vibration numbers.

Since ancient times the correlation between numerical proportion and sound effect, which may be observed here, has fascinated theorists. The simplest of proportions in vibrations (1:2 and 2:3) produce the octave and the fifth, which we know through aural experience to be the simplest and purest concords. This same relationship continues through the other intervals; the more complex the ratios of the vibrations, the more complex and discordant are the sounds.

Every interval may be found at some point within the theoretically infinite partial series. In our own music we make particular use of certain combinations which occur within the first seventeen partials, relying especially on the simplicity and understandability of the consonant intervals at the beginning of the series. The diagram on page 211 shows the tone A (110 vibrations) with all its partials up to the seventeenth. The series is given in musical notation, in terms of string divisions, vibration frequencies, intervals, proportions, and sizes in cents. Tones which are not used in our music because their intonation conflicts with the kind we consider normal are shown as black notes. Our notation can express these tones only approximately with the help of plus and minus signs, which indicate slight (less than a normal half-step) deviations in the pitches. The odd intervals produced by combinations involving these "out of tune" notes are placed in parentheses. At the bottom of the diagram, the sizes of intervals on keyboard instruments using twelve-tone equal temperament are given in cents, for comparison with the sizes normally used in singing and playing untempered instruments.

Besides the vibrating string, there are several other important sources for the tones produced by musical instruments. Actually these sources are employed not singly but in combinations to generate the individual tone qualities of the instruments. With some references to the most frequently used combinations, we shall treat each of the remaining sources separately.

EDGE-TONE

Edge-tone is produced when a stream of air passes rapidly at a certain critical angle over an edge, such as the top of a bottle or the blow hole of a flute. The air on the other side of the edge forms into *whorls*, which are areas of higher air pressure. The whorls and the low areas between them produce cycles, which may be heard as tone.

THE PARTIAL SERIES

Partial numbers	1	2	3	4	5	6	7	8	9	10	11	12	13	14	15	16	17
String divisions	1	$\frac{1}{2}$	$\frac{1}{3}$	$\frac{1}{4}$	$\frac{1}{5}$	$\frac{1}{6}$	$\frac{1}{7}$	$\frac{1}{8}$	$\frac{1}{9}$	$\frac{1}{10}$	$\frac{1}{11}$	$\frac{1}{12}$	$\frac{1}{13}$	$\frac{1}{14}$	$\frac{1}{15}$	$\frac{1}{16}$	$\frac{1}{17}$
Frequencies	110	220	330	440*	550	660	770	880	990	1100	1210	1320	1430	1540	1650	1760	1870

Intervals (between adjacent partials):

Intervals	8	5	4	M 3	m 3	(m 3 −)(M 2 +)	M 2	M 2	(M 2 −)(m 2 +)	(m 2 +)(M 2 −)	(M 2 −)(m 2 +)	m 2	m 2
Proportions	1:2	2:3	3:4	4:5	5:6	(6:7)	(7:8)	8:9	9:10	(10:11)	(11:12)	(12:13)	(13:14)	(14:15)	15:16	16:17
Sizes in cents	1200	702	498	386	316	267	231	204	182	165	150	139	128	120	112	106

Intervals between non-adjacent partials (sizes calculated by adding those of known intervals— e.g. a 4 is 498, and a M3 is 386. These intervals superimposed give a M6 of 884).

M 6 Prop. 3:5 Size 884

m 6 Prop. 5:8 Size 814

M 7 Prop. 8:15 Size 1088

m 7 Prop. 5:9 Size 1018

702 Fifth (2:3)
− 112 Half-step (15:16)
590 Aug. fourth (32:45)

498 Fourth (3:4)
+ 112 Half-step (15:16)
610 Dim. Fifth (45:64)

None of tritones above is used in "natural" intonation. The size must be determined by context, and by addition or subtraction involving intervals of clearly understood sizes. Fourths and fifths plus or minus leading tone half-steps are one method of derivation. By proportions the tritones evolved are very complex.

*The frequency 440 for the A is an arbitrary selection by the American Federation of Musicians. In Europe 435 has been used (called International Pitch).

Intervals of the 12-tone equal temperament shown in cents. (Compare with natural sizes given above.)

Interval	8	5	4	M 6	M 3	m 3	m 6	m 7	M 7	M 2	m 2	T
Cents	1200	700	500	900	400	300	800	1000	1100	200	100	600

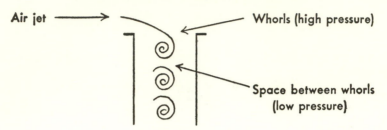

Edge-tone is always coupled to other sources which increase its volume and richness. The flute, the orchestral instrument which relies most extensively on edge-tone, reinforces it with an air column.

REEDS

Pieces of cane cut to certain thicknesses and shapes may be the vibrating agencies which produce tone. In the clarinet a single piece of cane is fastened to the mouthpiece (this is the reason the clarinet is called a *single-reed instrument*). When air is forced against the end of the reed, the reed expands away from the firm mouthpiece, and a puff of air passes through, forming a whorl on the other side. The resiliency of the reed causes it to contract somewhat, reducing the flow of air, and forming a low-pressure area behind the whorl. These events, the expansion and contraction of the reed, give rise to a cycle:

Single reed lies flat against the mouth-piece.	Reed expands to al-low a puff of air to enter.	Reed contracts, re-ducing the flow of air.

In the oboe, two pieces of cane tied together at one end are the vibrating agents (this is the reason the oboe is called a *double-reed instrument*). Air is forced against the two reeds, which at first expand, letting a puff of air pass through, and then contract, reducing the supply of air. These events, as with the single reed, give rise to a cycle:

Double reeds lie flat   Reeds expand.   Reeds contract
together.   again.

The lips, held firm against the mouthpiece of a brass instrument, may themselves function as double reeds.

AIR COLUMNS

All wind instruments employ in common one source of tone: a tube or pipe of some sort which contains a column of air. This column of air is set in motion by the whorls which enter it from the blow hole, mouthpiece, or reed. According to the shape of the column, the air assumes various patterns of activity, and the patterns, in turn, account for the sort of tone quality produced by the pipe.

The outsides of the pipes of most instruments appear to be cylindrical in shape. But the bore of the inside is sometimes cylindrical, and sometimes conical:

Cylindrical bore   Conical bore

A pipe which has a conical bore will produce a full supply of partials, and so, likewise, will a cylindrical pipe if it is open at both ends. But if one end of a cylindrical pipe is closed, it produces only the odd-numbered partials (1, 3, 5, etc.), and its pitch is not the same as an open pipe of equal length.

The pitches of open and closed cylindrical pipes are different because the nodes and antinodes form differently. Nodes and antinodes in this instance are areas of lower or higher molecular activity of the air within the pipes. In open pipes the air at the ends is active, forming antinodes, while a node forms in the middle. In closed pipes the node forms at the closed end.

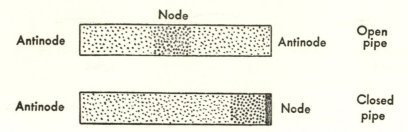

The pitch of the pipe is determined by the *wave length* it produces; and this, in turn, is dependent on the positions of the nodes. The formula for determining the wave length of an open or closed cylindrical pipe is: *the distance from node to antinode times four.* If the above open and closed pipes were each two feet long, the distance from node to antinode in the first pipe would be one foot, and the length of the wave would be four feet. The distance from node to antinode in the second pipe would be two feet, and the length of the wave would be eight feet.

Wave length, like string length, *is inversely proportional to frequency.* Therefore, if a wave length of four feet were to produce a frequency of 132 cycles, a wave length of eight feet would produce a frequency of 66 cycles.

The air in pipes divides into partials just as the vibrating string does. The nodes and antinodes described above account for only the fundamental sounds of cylindrical pipes. The next subdivisions are:

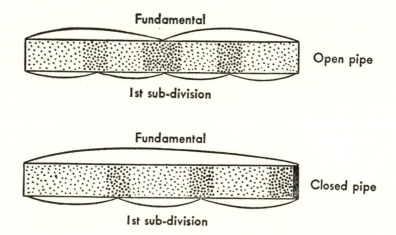

The first subdivision of the open pipe is in wave lengths one half as large as that of the fundamental. Since frequency is inversely proportional to wave length, the frequency of the first subdivision is twice that of the fundamental, corresponding to the second partial of a vibrating string (the octave above the fundamental).

The first subdivision of the closed pipe produces lengths one third as large as the fundamental. Calculating by the same principle, the frequency would be three times that of the fundamental. This produces the pitch a twelfth above the fundamental, corresponding to the third partial of a vibrating string. This explains the fact stated earlier that closed cylindrical pipes produce only the odd-numbered partials of the partial series.

The nodal distributions of conical pipes cannot be diagrammed with the clarity and simplicity which is possible with the cylindrical pipes. It suffices to note that the pitch production of a conical pipe will be the same as that of an open cylindrical pipe of the same length. Perhaps the relationships between the pitch-producing characteristics of the three kinds of pipes may be made clearer by the following diagram. All three of these pipes will produce the same pitch:

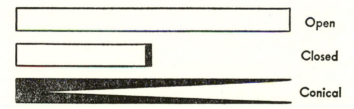

Open

Closed

Conical

MEMBRANES AND PLATES

Vibrating membranes or plates (metal or wood) are the principal sound-producing agents for most percussion instruments. Membranes are used on such instruments as drums and the tambourine, while plates are used in round form for gongs and cymbals, and in oblong form for the glockenspiel, celesta, and xylophone. Plates are also important in the tone-producing systems of many nonpercussion instruments; in the form of "sounding boards," or made into boxes of various shapes, they reinforce the tones of the piano, harp, violin, and other bowed or plucked instruments.

The only instrument of clear and definite pitch using a stretched membrane is the kettledrum. While the pitch of the fundamental is definite, the tone still has some of the characteristics of a noise. Here is a diagram showing how some of the nodal lines form on the drumhead. Note from the figures that the partials are not exact multiples of the fundamental.

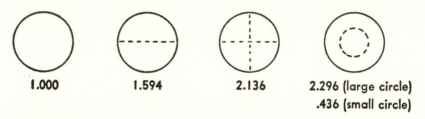

| 1.000 | 1.594 | 2.136 | 2.296 (large circle)
.436 (small circle) |

The distribution of the nodal lines in other round-shaped membranes or plates would somewhat resemble that for the kettledrum, but the partials would be even less close to the proportions of the normal series.

The oblong plates of metal or wood which are used in the glockenspiel, celesta, and xylophone assume nodal patterns similar to those of vibrating strings.

Chimes are open metal tubes which combine platelike vibration with that of the air column inside.

Actual bells have always been an acoustical mystery. The partials of bells are not entirely regular, and the strike-note is not the fundamental itself. It has been claimed that the strike-note of a good bell is an octave below the fifth partial, but why this particular tone happens to sound has never been satisfactorily explained.

APPENDIX

✠ 2 ✠

Instruments of the Orchestra: Some Features of Notation and Technique

One of the main functions of an introductory music theory text is to deal with problems of notation and reading. These matters have been dealt with in a general way in the preceding chapters, but we may now devote some additional and more specialized attention to the notation and reading problems which occur in the most complicated sort of musical writing: orchestral scores. In these complex musical documents the parts for some instruments may be written in one key, while the parts for others are in different keys, and there are many special instructions to the players which may alter the expected sounds of the instruments. In no other situation is musical notation in such an indirect relation to the actual sound.

Learning to read a score the way a conductor must be able to read one is an advanced aspect of practical musicianship, and naturally comes at a very late point in musical training. But it is nevertheless true that no student (not even musically untutored ones taking history or "appreciation" courses) fails to encounter scores in some way almost from the time of his earliest training in music. He finds, or is told, that the visual impression received by following a score as he listens will help him to understand the music. In a general sort of way, it apparently does provide such help. But it would provide more, no doubt, if the student were able not only to follow the vague shapes and groupings of the instrumental parts on the page, but to take the score to the piano and play slowly through certain passages which may excite his curiosity.

The problems which make score-reading a special and difficult task even for an otherwise musically literate student are not confined only to the huge scores of the late nineteenth century or to contemporary works; these problems occur even in the relatively simple classical scores of Haydn and Mozart. For example, a student who looks at the score of such a familiar work as Mozart's Symphony in G Minor will see there an indication that the horn parts are in B♭ alto. How is he to know exactly what this means, and how it will affect the sound in relation to the notes he sees written on the page?

Of course, information of this kind can be found in books on orchestration. The purpose of this appendix, however, is to present such information in compact form, in a context which does not include so much of the mass of other technical data that, by necessity, a book on orchestration must contain. Along with providing assistance to the student in the preliminary problems of score-reading, this appendix will also extend somewhat the treatment of two other basic matters mentioned briefly in the body of the text: articulation (and the means of notating it) on the various kinds of instruments, and the instrumental uses of the various clefs. It may, in addition, support the suggestion in Chapter 15 that Experiment 59 be treated as a lesson in instrumentation as well as melody-writing.

STRINGED INSTRUMENTS

Within any ten pages of fairly elaborate orchestration it is almost certain that the string parts will contain more indications and symbols to direct the performer than will be found in the parts for any other group of instruments. These markings indicate the styles of bowing, certain kinds of fingering, and various special effects not used in ordinary playing. Their profuseness is a natural reflection of the stringed instrument's flexibility and wide range of possible effects.

BOWING

The phrasing slurs in string parts do not necessarily indicate the punctuation of the units of musical form; they only indicate, specifically, the number of tones to be played in one stroke of the bow. The directions of the strokes are indicated (when necessary) by the signs ⊓ for *downbow* and ∨ for *upbow:*

In the above example, each of the circled groups of tones may sound smoothly connected (Italian: *legato*) even though the slurring divides each group into two bow strokes. Phrasing, in other words, is independent of bowing in string music, and the slur marks do not necessarily indicate separately articulated groups of tones. Since, by intention, the bowing sequence is irregular (not just downbow, upbow), bowing signs have been placed above the notes.

Dots (or wedges) placed next to the note-heads in string parts indicate some form of *staccato* (Italian: detached), or *non legato* execution. The notes are articulated separately, as though a short rest were inserted between them.

Dashes next to the note-heads (tenuto marks) may not necessarily indicate a prolongation of the notes (see page 52), but instead, a semi-legato articulation, with very slight separations between the notes.

Various bowings, indicated by dots, dashes, or combinations of dots or dashes with slurs, are listed below, together with the foreign terms which are used to identify them:

1. *Détaché* (Fr.). Separate bow strokes for each note. Notation: no slurs.

VIOLIN

Sing.,   plur.
It.   violino, violini
Fr.   violon, violons
Ger. Violine, Violinen

VIOLA

Sing., plur.
It.   viola, viole
Fr.   alto, altos
Ger. Bratsche, Bratschen

Tuning

Tuning

Approximate upper range limits in orchestral usage:

1. Violin. Two octaves above the highest string.
2. Viola. ⎫ A twelfth above the highest string.
3. Cello. ⎭
4. Double-bass. An octave above the highest string.

INSTRUMENTS

CELLO

Sing.,   *plur.*
It.   violoncello, violoncelli
Fr.   violoncelle, violoncelles
Ger. Violoncell, Violoncelle

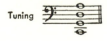

DOUBLE-BASS

Sing.,   *plur.*
It.   contrabasso, contrabassi
Fr.   contre basse, contre basses
Ger. Kontrabass, Kontrabässe

(Sounds an octave lower)

2. *Martelé* (Fr.), *Martellato* (It.). A "hammered" détaché stroke made with strong pressure near the tip of the bow. Notation: staccato dots, or wedges.

3. *Spiccato, Saltato* (It.), *Sautillé* (Fr.). The resiliency of the bow hair and stick are employed to keep the bow bouncing off the string between the notes. Notation: staccato dots next to the note-heads.

4. *Staccato* (It.) Besides its general meaning, this word may refer to a specific bow stroke. The bow is made, by a series of increased pressures from the bow hand, to produce staccato accents on each note. This process takes place while the bow is moving in one direction. In some cases, when moving upbow, the bow may jump from the string between notes (*staccato volante*, or "flying staccato"). Notation for either kind of staccato: dots with slurs, which indicate when the direction of the bow should be changed:

5. *Portato* (It.), *Louré* (Fr.). Dashes (tenuto marks) instead of dots with slurs indicate a semi-legato stroke, with a number of notes played in one direction of the bow:

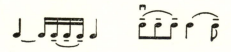

6. *Ricochet, Jeté* (Fr.). A number of tones are played on the rebounding motions of the bow after it has been dropped on the string, usually moving in the direction of the downbow. Notation: like staccato, dots with slurs:

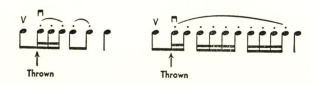

7. *Tremolo* (Italian: "trembling"). Many unmeasured fast strokes on the same tone. This effect is shown in notation by the use of many strokes across the note-stem. Unless the number of strokes is considerable, confusion may arise with a type of abbreviation which indicates definite divisions of long notes by strokes across the stems (see Appendix IV, page 272).

FINGERING

Ordinarily indications of fingering are not found in orchestral scores; the choice of fingering is left to the player. There are, however, a few special cases in which fingering indications are inserted, and there are also certain unusual kinds of left-hand technique which affect the notation, and therefore may be appropriately mentioned here. Some fingering indications and some of the less usual kinds of left-hand technique are included in the following list:

1. *Characteristic Tone Colors.* Each string has a tone color different from the others. Composers occasionally desire the tone color of a specific string. This is indicated by a mark such as *Sul A* (Italian: "on the A string"), followed by a broken line. All the tones under the line are to be played on the indicated string.

2. *Double-stops.* While the stringed instruments are primarily melodic instruments, playing only one note at a time, a technique known

as double-stopping involves playing on two strings at once. A further extension of this technique may involve three- or four-note chords.

Sometimes a section of strings, which usually plays together on a single melodic line, will be required to play two or more separate lines, dividing itself into groups. The indication in such cases will be: *Divisi* (It.), *Divisé* (Fr.), *Geteilt* (Ger.).

Since divisi parts are sometimes written on one stave, and look like passages involving double-stopping, real double-stopping is clearly indicated by the negative term *non divisi*.

3. *Open Strings.* When no fingers are placed on the fingerboard, the open strings (those to which the instrument is tuned) are allowed to sound. The tone of the open strings is brighter than that of the fingered notes, and there may be occasions when their distinctive quality is desired by the composer. Also, certain complex passages may require open strings for purely technical reasons. Open strings are indicated by little zeros placed above the notes:

4. *Natural Harmonics.* If the nodal points on the string are touched lightly (not pressed down to the fingerboard), natural harmonics are produced. When the sounding pitch is the same as the written pitch, little zeros (as with open strings) are placed above the notes. The following diagram shows the nodal position and notation of the second partial on the A string:

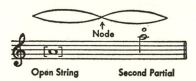

If the sounding note does not agree in pitch with the written note (which shows the spot on the string to be touched lightly by the finger), the written note is diamond-shaped. Here are the nodal points and notations for the third partial on the A string. In one position, the diamond-shaped note is used; and in the other, a zero is placed over the note:

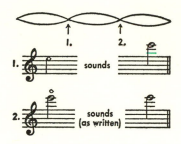

5. *Artificial Harmonics.* One finger plays a stopped note while another finger touches the string lightly a fourth higher. The tones produced are two octaves higher than the stopped note (fourth partials). The stopped note is written normally, but the point touched lightly is shown by a diamond-shaped note. The two notes may be connected on one stem (not to be confused with double-stops).

6. *Vibrato.* The feature of technique which accounts more than any other for the close resemblance between string tone and the

singing voice is the *vibrato*. The ball of the finger is made to rotate by means of hand and arm movements to produce a rapid alternate lowering and raising of the pitch, corresponding to the vibrating sound of a freely produced vocal tone. The use of vibrato in string playing is taken for granted, and does not require an indication. But for certain quiet effects, the less colorful sound of unvibrated tones may be desired, and in these cases the indication *senza vibrato* may occur.

SPECIAL EFFECTS

Certain techniques and devices may produce special effects in which the normal sound of the instrument is drastically altered. Some of these effects are:

1. *Pizzicato* (Italian: "plucked"). A finger of the bow hand usually does the plucking. In special cases, the fingers of the left hand may pluck. When notes plucked by the left hand are in close juxtaposition with bowed notes, they are indicated by little crosses placed above the tones.

2. *Sul ponticello* (It.), *Au chevalet* (Fr.), *Am Steg* (Ger.): "on the bridge." A whistling effect caused by bowing too near the bridge with insufficient pressure. The fundamental is obscured by the confused whistling of high partials.

3. *Sul tastiera, sul tasto* (It.), *Sur la touche* (Fr.), *Am Griffbrett* (Ger.): "on the fingerboard." The bow is applied over the fingerboard, too far from the bridge. The effect is the opposite of ponticello. The sound is softened, and lacks overtones. Because the sound is flutelike, the terms *flautando* and *flautato* are sometimes used.

4. *Col legno* (It.): "with the wood." The bow stick is struck against the strings.

After "sul ponticello," "sul tastiera," or "col legno" the terms *Naturale* (It.), *Naturel* (F.), and *Natürlich* (Ger.) indicate the return to normal playing.

A special effect which is neither a fingering nor a bowing device is:

5. *Con sordini* (It.), *Avec les sourdines* (Fr.), *Mit Dämpfern* (Ger.): "with mutes" (also given in the singular). Mutes for stringed

instruments are clamplike objects of wood, metal, or rubber which are placed on the bridge (or on the strings just behind the bridge) to reduce the volume and brilliance of the sound. Terms such as *Senza sordino* (It.), *Ôtez les sourdines* (F.), or *Dämpfern ab* (Ger.) indicate the removal of the mutes.

OTHER TERMS

There are a few other terms which are commonly found in the string parts of orchestral scores, and which seem more appropriately listed here than in the glossary of foreign terms (Appendix IV, page 258). These terms are:

A punta d'arco (It.).
Au point d'archet (Fr.). } At the point of the bow.
An der Spitze (Ger.).

Al tallone (It.).
Au talon (Fr.). } At the "nut," "frog," or "heel" of the bow.
Am Frosche (Ger.).

Metà (It.).
Moitié (Fr.). } Only half of the section of instruments plays.
Die Hälfte (Ger.).

Tutti (It.).
Tout (Fr.). } All the instruments play.
Alle (Ger.).

THE HARP

The modern harp has strings which are tuned to the diatonic scale of C♭ major, from ‚C♭ to g♭′′′′. There are seven pedals at the base of the harp, each of which may raise one of the diatonic tones of the scale, in all octaves, by a half-step, or by a whole-step. One pedal, for instance, can raise all the C-flats to C-naturals or C-sharps; another can raise all the D-flats to D-naturals or D-sharps, and so forth.

Since an individual tone cannot be raised to a natural or sharp without changing the same tone in all other octaves, the harp offers some resistance to chromatic styles. Its notation, too, is sometimes very strange-looking, as technical considerations (changes of ped-

HARP

It. Arpa
Fr. Harpe
Ger. Harfe

Range
and
Tunings

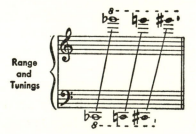

als) may suggest enharmonic notations which have no apparent relation to the spelling of the music in other parts of the orchestra.

Harp music, like that for the piano, is notated on two staves with treble and bass clefs, connected by a brace.

Special effects encountered in harp parts are:

1. *The Glissando*. The strings are set to a given chord or scale, and the hands are brushed over the strings. The basic notes are usually indicated without rhythm, and wavy lines and the word "glissando" fill the space on the staff.

2. *Harmonics*. Little zeros above the notes in harp parts indicate that these tones are harmonics. The tones sound one octave above the notated pitch, as they are second partials produced by touching the node in the middle of the string with part of the hand while a finger of the same hand plucks.

WOODWIND INSTRUMENTS
Nontransposing Instruments
PICCOLO · FLUTE · OBOE
BASSOON · CONTRABASSOON

The parts for these instruments of the woodwind family are more direct and simple in notation than those for any other members of the orchestra. The notation is at actual pitch (the piccolo and contrabassoon are partial exceptions), and the slurs, dots, and dashes which occur are reproduced with great exactness. Legato is obtained simply by playing on an unbroken stream of air, while a technique known as *tonguing*, in which the tip of the tongue is placed against the teeth or reed to stop the flow of air, can produce any degree of staccato.

The slur-line covers all tones to be played legato. Staccatos are shown by means of dots (wedges are rare in wind-instrument parts). Tenuto marks over the notes indicate semi-legato. Semi-legato is also indicated by a slur-line over dots or dashes, unlike in string notation.

"Special effects" are not as common to these instruments as they are to the strings and to some brass instruments. The only one likely to be encountered (generally in flute parts) is called *flutter-tonguing* (Ger., *Flatterzunge*). The tongue flutters as in rolling the letter R,

WOODWIND

PICCOLO

It. Flauto piccolo
      (or Ottavino)
Fr. Petite Flûte
Ger. Kleine Flöte

(Sounds an octave higher.)

FLUTE

Sing., *plur.*
It.   Flauto, flauti
Fr.   Flûte, flûtes
Ger. Flöte, Flöten

(some instruments)

INSTRUMENTS

OBOE

Sing.,   plur.
It.   Oboe, oboi
Fr.   Hautbois, hautbois
Ger. Oboe, Oboen
       (in old scores, "Hoboe[n]")

ENGLISH HORN

It.   Corno Inglese
Fr.   Cor Anglais
Ger. Englisches Horn

WOODWIND

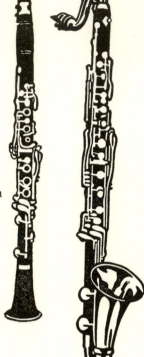

CLARINET

Sing.,   *plur.*

It.   Clarinetto, clarinetti
      (or Clarino, clarini)
Fr.   Clarinette, clarinettes
Ger. Klarinette, Klarinetten

BASS CLARINET

It.   Clarinetto Basso
      (or Clarone)
Fr.   Clarinette Basse
Ger. Bassklarinette

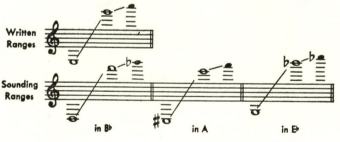

INSTRUMENTS (continued)

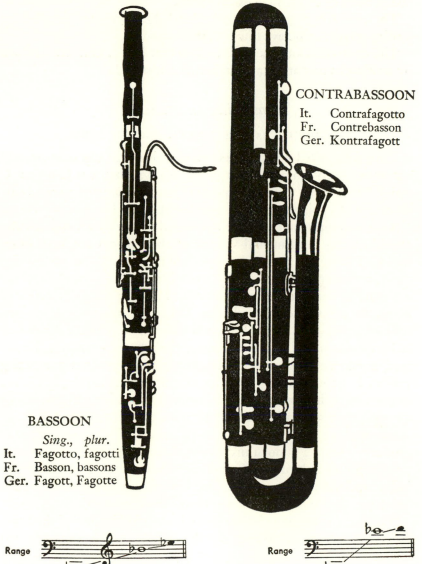

CONTRABASSOON

It.   Contrafagotto
Fr.   Contrebasson
Ger. Kontrafagott

BASSOON

Sing., plur.
It.   Fagotto, fagotti
Fr.   Basson, bassons
Ger. Fagott, Fagotte

Range

Range
(Sounds an octave lower)

and the articulation is blurred. This effect is a modern one: there are no instances of its use in classical scores.

The piccolo's range is so high that ledger lines are avoided by writing its part an octave lower than it sounds.

The contrabassoon's range is so low that ledger lines are avoided by writing its part an octave higher than it sounds.

Transposing Instruments

CLARINET . BASS CLARINET . ENGLISH HORN

If we were asked what is the normal scale of the piano, we would say immediately, thinking of the white keys, that it is C major. C major has become a normal, neutral key because the major scale starting at this point requires no accidentals.

Some wind instruments are constructed so that their natural scales (based on the fundamental sounds of their pipes) are keys other than C. The feeling that the natural scale should be C is so strong that these instruments' natural scales are written as C, even though the sounding pitches are entirely different. For example, the clarinet in B♭ has B♭ major as its natural scale. When the player sees a written scale of C major, he plays his natural scale (B♭), with the result that all his tones sound a whole-step lower than they are written. Therefore, should a composer wish a clarinet in B♭ to produce a sounding scale of C, he would have to write the part a tone higher, in D. We can say, then, that a transposing instrument is one for which C-major notation expresses a natural scale on some tone other than C.

Clarinets are also constructed in A and E♭. The instrument in A produces a scale a minor third lower than C; therefore its notation must be a minor third higher than the actual sound. The instrument in E♭ produces a scale a minor third higher than C; therefore its notation must be a minor third lower than the actual sound.

The part for the bass clarinet in B♭ is written like that of the regular B♭ clarinet, in treble clef, but the actual sound is a major ninth lower.

The English horn, the alto of the oboe family, is in F. Written C major sounds F major, a fifth lower; therefore the notation must be a fifth higher than the actual sound.

In matters of articulation, these transposing woodwinds are notated just as clearly as the nontransposing instruments mentioned above.

BRASS INSTRUMENTS

All of the brass instruments have undergone changes in mechanism or size during the period of our standard literature, and, since many of these changes have affected their notations, we shall include some of their historical backgrounds in the following discussions.

The Trumpet and Cornet

In its basic form, the trumpet has a history which extends back into antiquity. It was originally played like the modern military bugle; the only tones it could produce were the partials above its one fundamental. In spite of this apparent limitation, the trumpet became a very prominent instrument in the baroque period (e.g., in the works of Bach); performers with highly specialized training learned to use the scalelike high partials in brilliant passages, which remain even today the trumpeter's most severe test.

In the latter part of the eighteenth century, a system of *crooks* (small extensions of tubing which could be inserted or removed) made it possible to change the fundamental of a trumpet, thereby providing a wider supply of notes for a single instrument. Shortly afterward, in the early nineteenth century, a system of valves was introduced, which made it possible to change the length of the tube with great rapidity by fingering. After the introduction of valves, the trumpet changed from a more or less tonally limited instrument to a chromatically fluent and flexible member of the modern orchestra.

Even after the introduction of valves, crooks continued to be used so that the basic key of the instrument could be varied when desired. The scores of standard literature contain (besides B♭ and C) trumpets in the following keys:

1. *Trumpet in A*—written a m3 higher than the actual sound, like the clarinet in A.
2. *Trumpet in B*—written a m2 higher than the actual sound.
3. *Trumpet in D*—written a M2 lower than the actual sound.
4. *Trumpet in E♭*—written a m3 lower than the actual sound.

5. *Trumpet in E*—written a M3 lower than the actual sound.

6. *Trumpet in F*—written a fourth lower than the actual sound.
(Not to be confused with French horn in F, to be discussed later.)

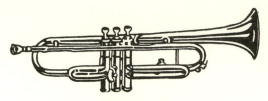

TRUMPET

Sing.,   plur.
It.   Tromba, trombe
Fr.   Trompette, trompettes
Ger. Trompete, Trompeten

CORNET

Sing.,   plur.
It.   Cornetto, cornetti
Fr.   Cornet à pistons
Ger. Kornett, Kornette

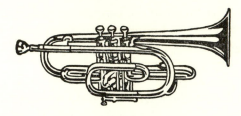

The trumpet is muted by a device which is inserted into the bell. The indications in foreign languages are the same as those given for stringed instruments.

All kinds of staccato articulations are possible on the trumpet—even very rapid ones. There are, however, fewer detailed indications of articulation in trumpet parts (in fact, brass parts in general) than for woodwinds. The marks that do occur have the same meanings as for woodwinds.

The *cornet* is similar to the trumpet, but has a more mellow sound, and even greater agility. It is found mainly in the scores of French composers (Bizet, Franck, etc.). The cornet in current use is in B♭, like the trumpet. In older scores other keys are found, and these transpositions are like those of the older trumpets.

The French Horn

An evolution through crooks and valves similar to that of the trumpet took place in the development of the French horn. The modern instrument is in F (written, as for the English horn, a fifth higher than the actual sound). In almost general use nowadays is a *double horn*, which combines with the F horn another length of tubing pitched in B♭, a fourth higher than F. The use of the B♭ section, however, does not affect the notation, which remains in F. The choice between the two units of the double horn is left entirely to the player.

The crooks used in the horns of the classical and romantic symphonies accounted for a great variety of key indications in the scores. Some of these keys (besides F) were:

1. *Horn in C*—written an octave above the actual sound.
2. *Horn in D*—written a m7 above the actual sound.
3. *Horn in E♭*—written a M6 above the actual sound.
4. *Horn in E*—written a m6 above the actual sound.
5. *Horn in G*—written a fourth above the actual sound.
6. *Horn in A*—written a m3 above the actual sound, like the clarinet in A.
7. *Horn in B♭ basso*—written a ninth above the actual sound, like the bass clarinet in B♭.
8. *Horn in B♭* (alto)—written a M2 above the actual sound, like the regular B♭ clarinet.

The horn uses both treble and bass clefs. In older scores (Bee-thoven, for example), the transposition is inverted when the bass clef is used. If the notes for a horn in F were written a fifth higher than the actual sound in the treble clef, they would be written a fourth lower than the actual sound in the bass clef. Likewise, a horn in B♭ basso written a M9 higher in the treble clef would be written a m7 lower in the bass clef.

FRENCH HORN (DOUBLE HORN)

Sing., plur.
It.   Corno, corni
Fr.   Cor, cors
Ger. Horn, Hörner

Low notes playable
on the B♭ section.

There are no unusual features of articulation for the horn. There are, however, certain special effects. These are:

1. *Stopped Horn* (It., *chiuso;* Fr., *bouché;* Ger., *gestopft*). The hand is pushed into the bell of the horn to produce a certain muffled but intense kind of sound. Any pitch alteration that may result from changing the length of the vibrating air column has to be taken care of by the player, who will transpose to cause the correct note to sound. Little crosses are placed over the stopped notes.

Stopped notes can be soft, which is not too different from the sound produced by a real mute, or very much forced, which produces a brutal sound usually called for by such words as *cuivré* (French: "brassy"), or *schmetternd* (German: "blaring").

2. *Muted Horn* (It., *con sordino;* Fr., *avec sourdine;* Ger., *mit Dämpfer*). An actual pear-shaped device is inserted into the bell. This device has holes which prevent complete stopping and the consequent change of pitch. The "brassy" effect may also be employed with the real mute.

3. The effect described above (cuivré, schmetternd) with stopped and muted horns may be employed as well with an open horn.

The Trombone

Unlike the trumpet and horn, the trombone has not changed in playing principles from the earliest forms we know (about the fifteenth century). Its slide mechanism, which produces a new fundamental in each position, gave it the tonal freedom from the beginning which the horn and trumpet acquired later through the use of valves.

The most common modern trombones are the regular *tenor trombone,* and an enlarged and extended form of this instrument called the *tenor-bass trombone.* The latter instrument is of larger bore than the regular tenor trombone, and is equipped with a tube extension operated by a valve, which makes certain low tones possible and offers the player a greater choice of slide positions for the high notes.

Parts for the tenor trombone were formerly written in tenor clef, at sounding pitch. Nowadays both tenor parts and the lower parts assigned to the tenor-bass trombone are written in bass clef, at sounding pitch.

Certain other trombones besides the tenor trombone are found in the scores of standard literature. They are:

1. *The Alto Trombone.* The range of this smaller instrument is a fourth higher than the tenor trombone. Parts are written in alto or bass clef, at sounding pitch.

2. *The Bass Trombone.* An instrument pitched a fourth below the tenor trombone. The parts are written in bass clef, at sounding pitch. This instrument has been superseded by the valve extension on the tenor trombone (tenor-bass trombone).

3. *The Double-bass Trombone.* Used by Wagner, this instrument has a range an octave below the tenor trombone. The parts are written in bass clef with ledger lines, at sounding pitch (not an octave higher as with the string double-bass, or the contrabassoon).

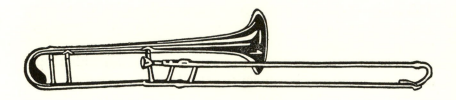

TROMBONE (TENOR)

	Sing.,	*plur.*
It.	Trombone,	tromboni
Fr.	Trombone,	trombones
Ger.	Posaune,	Posaunen

Range

Playable on the tenor-bass trombone.

Theoretically, the trombone cannot play legato. Unless the player uses his tongue to stop the flow of air between many of the notes, the smearing sounds of the slide changes can be heard. However, good trombone players manage to produce a legato impression when they desire it. Articulation marks, again, are usually less sensitive than for woodwind instruments.

The trombone can use a mute (inserted into the bell), which is indicated by the foreign terms already cited for strings.

The Tuba

Like the trombone, the tuba is not a transposing instrument. But it exists in several sizes with different fundamentals and ranges. The two most important sizes for orchestral music are the *bass tuba* in F or E♭, and the *double-bass tuba* in B♭ (called the "double B flat," or BB♭ bass tuba). Tuba players use these instruments interchangeably, and only at the less common extreme limits is there a significant difference in their ranges. Score readers need not be too much concerned as to which instrument the part will be played on; most scores are vague on this point, often saying only, "tuba."

Some scores call for a *tenor tuba, euphonium,* or *baryton* (Ger.). This instrument is in B♭, and has a range an octave higher than the BB♭ tuba. Parts intended for this instrument adapt poorly, or may be impossibly high for the commoner bass tubas.

The name *helicon* (Greek: *helikós*, "coiled") is sometimes applied to tubas built in coiled form to be carried on the shoulder. A tuba with a forward-pointing bell was introduced by John Philip Sousa, and is called a *sousaphone*.

TUBAS

TENOR TUBA (EUPHONIUM)

It.	Eufonio	
Fr.	Basse à pistons	} in B♭
Ger.	Baryton	

BASS TUBA

It.	Tuba	
Fr.	Tuba	} in F or E♭
Ger.	Basstuba	

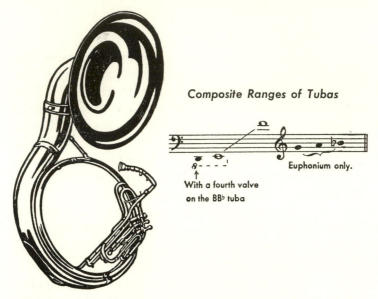

Composite Ranges of Tubas

With a fourth valve
on the BB♭ tuba

Euphonium only.

DOUBLE-BASS or BB♭ TUBA (SOUSAPHONE)

The parts for the bass and double-bass tubas are not written an octave higher than they sound, but in their actual ranges, using as many ledger lines as are necessary.

Elegance of articulation and special effects are, needless to say, reduced to a minimum with these heavy instruments.

The exceptions to the rule that tuba parts are nontransposing are found in certain works of Wagner. His *Ring of the Nibelungen* calls for a whole family of "tubas" (really constructed somewhat on the principles of horns) in various keys, which do transpose. Their keys are as follows:

1. *Tenor Tubas in B♭*, written a tone higher than the actual sound, or *tenor tubas in E♭*, written a M6 higher than the actual sound.

2. *Bass Tubas in F*, written a fifth higher than the actual sound, or *bass tubas in B♭*, written a M9 above the actual sound.

Wagner also wrote for a *contrabass tuba* in C, written at sounding pitch.

PERCUSSION INSTRUMENTS

Kettledrums

These drums are always used at least in pairs, and in some instances in groups of three or four. The calfskin membrane (the *head*) stretched over the top of the kettlelike metal body of the drum (the *shell*) can be brought to different degrees of tension, and when it is struck it produces a tone of definite pitch. Kettledrums used to be tuned exclusively by turning handles placed along the rim. Composers would choose certain important notes in the key of the piece (e.g., the tonic and dominant), and the player would prepare his instrument in advance. He could make changes in the tuning during the piece if allowed enough measures of rest. The invention of a pedal device for mechanical tuning makes it possible for the modern

A KETTLEDRUM with PEDAL

It.   Timpani ⎫ All plural forms, since kettledrums are
Fr.   Timbales ⎬ always used at least in pairs.
Ger. Pauken ⎭

Diameters of
the drumheads   30″   28″   25″   23″

Ranges (approx.)

kettledrum player to make very rapid changes. Since the introduction of pedals, kettledrum parts are no longer limited to a few important notes.

Orchestral scores indicate the exact tuning for hand-tuned kettledrums by letters, or by a small staff with the actual notes, placed in the margin at the start of the piece (see examples on pages 254 and 255). Changes of tuning are indicated along the staff, as needed, by the term "muta in ——" (Italian: *muta*, "change").

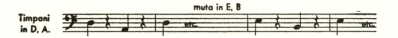

In modern scores, which assume pedal tuning, no advance pitch indication is needed.

A special device in kettledrum parts is the *roll*, indicated by the sign tr ⌇⌇⌇ above the notes. The effect is similar to the string tremolo,* consisting actually of very rapid repeated notes, accomplished by striking the drum alternately with each stick.

The roll, indicated in the same manner, is also employed on all other percussion instruments except those with keyboards.

The rare effect of muted kettledrums (It., *coperti*, "covered") used to be obtained by placing a cloth over the drumhead. Drumsticks tipped with sponge rather than felt provide a newer method of muting.

Other Drums

Like the kettledrum, the other instruments of the drum family have calfskin heads. But the shells of these drums are not built to resonate as they do for the kettledrum, the pitch is not as clear, and no tuning (of the deliberate kind used on the kettledrum) is possible.

The *side drum*, or *snare drum*, has two heads stretched on the front and back of a small metal shell. The head on the back has wire strings stretched across it, called *snares*. The snares vibrate when the top head (*batter-head*) is struck with wooden drumsticks. Loosening the snares "mutes" the snare drum.

* The tremolo notation (𝄑, many lines across the note-stem) is used in some scores.

The *tenor drum* is a deeper instrument than the snare drum. It has a wooden shell, not equipped with snares.

The *bass drum* is the largest member of the drum family. It is usually played with a single stick, covered at the end with a soft felt knob.

The *tambourin* (or *tambourin de Provence*), sometimes called for in French scores, is a drum with a shell which is very deep in relation to the head (deeper than the tenor drum). Don't confuse this drum with the "tambourine," which is discussed below (page 251).

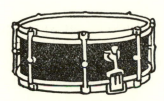

SNARE DRUM

It.   Tamburo Militare
Fr.   Tambour Militaire
Ger. Kleine Trommel

TENOR DRUM

It.   Cassa Rullante
Fr.   Caisse Rulante
Ger. Rührtrommel

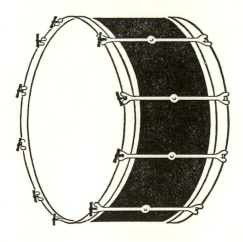

BASS DRUM

It.   Gran Cassa
Fr.   Grosse Caisse
Ger. Grosse Trommel

In Italian terminology the words *tamburo* and *cassa*, meaning "drum," are interchangeable. The same is true of the French words *caisse* and *tambour*.

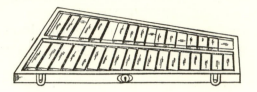

The Glockenspiel

It.   Campanelli
Fr.   Jeu de Timbres, or Carillon
Ger. Glockenspiel

This instrument consists of oblong steel plates of lengths graduated to give a chromatic scale, and arranged like a piano keyboard. It is played with a pair of wooden, rubber, or composition hammers. Some instruments have hollow resonators below the plates to enlarge the sound.

The usual range of the glockenspiel covers a span of two octaves and a fourth or fifth, although there are some smaller instruments with shorter ranges. In standard usage, the part for the glockenspiel is written two octaves below the actual sound (occasionally scores have the part written only one octave lower, which is recognizable by the extremely high range of the part):

Written Range
(sounds two
octaves higher)

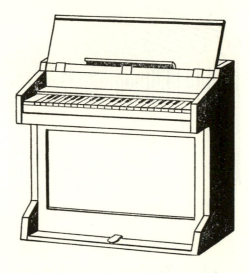

The Celesta

The celesta is a kind of glockenspiel equipped with a keyboard mechanism similar to that of the piano. The metal plates are coupled together with resonating boxes, so that the tone is more mellow than that of the glockenspiel. The part is written on two staves, like the piano, at one octave below the actual pitch:

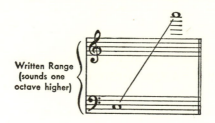

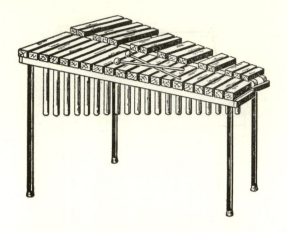

The Xylophone

It.   Xylofono, or Sylofono
Fr.   Xylophone
Ger. Xylophon

Except that its plates are made of wood rather than steel, the xylophone closely resembles the glockenspiel; it, too, is played with a pair of small hammers. The range of a small xylophone is:

Other larger instruments may extend this range upwards to f ′′′, or c ′′′′. Some of the larger instruments have resonators under the wooden plates.

Sometimes xylophone parts are written at sounding pitch rather than one octave lower. The actual sounding range is perhaps less important with the xylophone than with the bright and clear glockenspiel or celesta; in fact, the tone quality of the wooden plates is such that a precise identification of the range of the fundamental sound is difficult. Because of this ambiguity, xylophone players frequently play their parts in higher or lower octaves, as they choose.

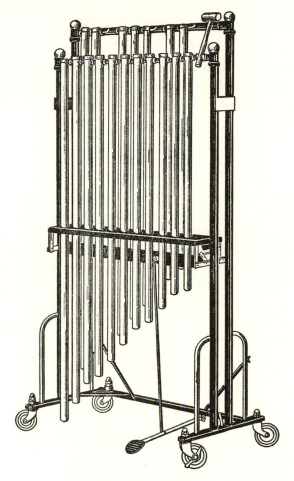

Chimes (Bells)

    It.   Campane
    Fr.   Cloches
    Ger. Glocken

Because real bells would be too heavy, and too difficult to mount on a concert platform, chimes are used when bell sounds are needed in the orchestra. Chimes are metal tubes hung from a frame, so that they vibrate freely when struck by a hammer. A complete set of chimes includes eighteen chromatic tones, filling in the following interval:

Written Range

Strong overtones may cause the written range of the chimes to sound one or two octaves higher.

Cymbals

It.   Piatti
Fr.   Cymbales
Ger. Becken

Cymbals are metal plates with small holes in the center through which straps are attached. When held by these straps, one in each hand, and crashed together, cymbals may produce one of the orchestra's loudest and most spectacular effects. This, however, is only one of a number of ways of playing them. Single cymbals can be played with hard drumsticks or kettledrum sticks to produce many different levels of volume and tone color. The bass drum and cymbal may be played by one person at the same time if one cymbal is mounted on the drum.

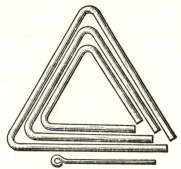

The Triangle

It.   Triangolo
Fr.   Triangle
Ger. Triangel

These are small steel rods bent into the shape their name implies. A triangle is suspended, and struck with a small straight metal rod (a "beater"). Its bright tinkle can be heard above the sound of the whole orchestra.

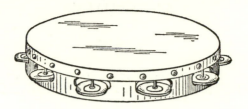

The Tambourine

It. Tambourino
Fr. Tambour de Basque
Ger. Schellentrommel, or Tambourin

The tambourine is a small drumlike instrument with slits in the side of the shell, within which are mounted loose metal plates called "jingles." The instrument can be played by shaking it, by striking the head, or by rubbing a moist thumb around the rim, which produces a roll as the jingles vibrate softly.

The Gong or Tam-Tam

The gong is an Oriental instrument, plate-shaped like a cymbal, but usually much larger. It is hung from a frame, and struck with a bass drumstick. The gong is not necessarily a loud instrument; soft sounds reverberate for a remarkably long time, and may produce very colorful effects.

Parts for the instruments of indefinite pitch do not actually require a staff, and some of them are occasionally written on a single line, without clef. But when a staff is used the high-pitched instruments (snare drum, tambourine, triangle) are nearly always shown with a treble clef. The bass drum is invariably shown with a bass clef, but the cymbals and gong may be seen with either bass or treble clef.

There is a final group of unclassifiable and rarely used percussion instruments, the titles of which explain themselves: they include gourds, rattles, and all kinds of exotic native instruments, as well as wind machines, pistols, taxi horns, typewriters, and anything else needed for the special occasion the composer may have had in mind.

APPENDIX

✠ 3 ✠

Examples from Orchestral Scores

The following excerpts from scores show, very sketchily, the development of the orchestra from the classical period to the present. Examine them carefully for some of the features of notation and instrumental technique mentioned in the preceding appendix. Try playing through each of the melodic lines for transposing instruments. Also try playing, very slowly, as many parts at once as your keyboard facility will allow.

1. The first page of the Symphony No. 7, Opus 92, by Ludwig
van Beethoven (1770–1827).

The instruments called for on the first page of this symphony are
more or less typical of the classical orchestra. Some of the scores of
Haydn and Mozart do not contain as many wind instruments as
shown here, while Beethoven's scores, on the other hand, sometimes
exceed this one by the addition of more horns (two more, four in
all), the piccolo, trombones (alto, tenor, and bass), or even the
contrabassoon.

2. The first page of the Symphony in D Minor, by César Franck (1822–90).

This symphony shows the more fully developed instrumentation of the romantic period. The "Cor anglais" and "Clarinette basse" were never used in classical symphonies. The horns are "Cors chromatiques," i.e., modern valve horns which do not have to use a variety of crooks. A typically French feature of this score is the use of cornets.

The harp, not indicated on this first page, has a prominent part in the second and third movements of this symphony.

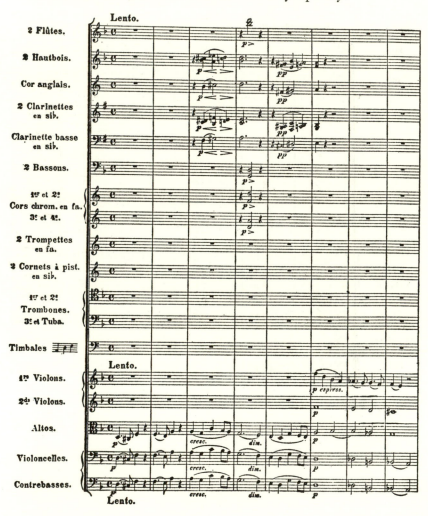

3. A page (small score, 236) from the last section of *Scheheraza-de*, by Nikolai Rimsky-Korsakov (1844–1908).*

This very colorful score is full of special instrumental effects. Here, all on one page, are artificial harmonics and pizzicato chords in the string parts, glissandos in the harp part, and examples of the use of cymbals and the triangle. The notation also uses several common abbreviations.

* Copyright by Edition M. P. Belaieff. Used by permission of Boosey & Hawkes, sole agents.

4. The beginning of the first variation of the *Philharmonic Variations*, by Paul Hindemith (born 1895).*

This page shows the full modern scoring for winds and strings. At this particular point in the piece the percussion is limited to timpani, and there is no harp. Except for the addition of various percussion instruments, modern scores are seldom larger than this. On the contrary, many of the most significant twentieth-century scores (by Hindemith, Stravinsky, Bartók, and others) call for considerably smaller instrumental combinations.

* Copyright 1932 by B. Schott's Soehne, Mainz; by permission of Associated Music Publishers, Inc.

APPENDIX

⚹4⚹

Foreign Musical Terms

The practice of adding verbal instructions and signs to musical notation in order to make the composer's intentions clearer began with the early baroque style, around 1600. Because of the prominence of Italian music during this period, Italian markings were adopted in countries other than Italy,* and gradually many of these markings lost their exclusively Italian identity: they formed a kind of international language of musical terms.

Indications of tempo and expression were quite sparse during the baroque period, but later in the eighteenth century, with the beginnings of the classical style, dynamics in particular assumed a new importance, and composers gave more detailed and specific indications of expression. A further increase in this phase of notation took place with the beginnings of Romanticism, and indications of character and expression became progressively more detailed as the musical style moved away from classical balance toward greater subjectivity or toward realism. In an effort to increase the effectiveness of verbal instructions about expression, and also in response to growing nationalistic tendencies, some composers in the second half of the nineteenth century abandoned Italian and began to use terms drawn from their native languages. Wagner in Germany, and Debussy in France were leaders in this direction: their much performed music has added dozens of new terms in German and French to the list that a well-educated musician needs to know.

Many contemporary composers have followed the trend established by Debussy and Wagner. Spanish composers have used Spanish; English and American composers have used English; and the

---

* The French baroque composers (Couperin, etc.) were the most notable exception. They used a rich vocabulary of terms from their own language.

257

Italians themselves have added new words freely, as though their language had never been the source for a frozen international vocabulary.

The growth of new terms in the three most used foreign languages (Italian, French, and German) has been so prolific in the last century that the limits for a useful glossary are very difficult to establish. Actually, any word appropriately used may become a musical term. One recent dictionary,* which says that it believes its list to be the most complete yet published, gives over 1,800 marks of expression and other terms relating to performance. The list given here includes about 450 terms, which would be, then, approximately 25 per cent of the number which might possibly have been included. Of these, about a hundred Italian terms are in everyday use, and are found in the most familiar works of the standard literature. The others make up a representative cross section of the less common Italian terms, and the newer ones introduced into musical usage by German and French composers. Although the list makes no pretense of being complete, it should serve as an adequate reference in most cases. For those few cases involving unusual terms not listed here, standard reference works may be consulted. Among these are:

1. *Harvard Dictionary of Music*, Willi Apel, Cambridge, Mass., 1951.
2. *The Concise Oxford Dictionary of Music*, Percy A. Scholes, Oxford, 1952.

Musical terms (as well as a great deal of other information) may also be found with somewhat less convenience in the following larger works:

3. *Grove's Dictionary of Music and Musicians.* London: The Macmillan Company, Fifth Edition, 1954.
4. *The Oxford Companion to Music*, Percy A. Scholes, Oxford. Ninth Edition, 1955.
5. *International Cyclopedia of Music and Musicians*, Oscar Thompson, Dodd, Mead & Company, 1952.

* *The Concise Oxford Dictionary of Music.*

GLOSSARY OF FOREIGN TERMS
RELATING TO PERFORMANCE

Abandonné (Fr.). "Negligent." Free rhythm.

Abbandono (It.). "Abandon." Free, passionate style.

A cappella (It.). "For the chapel," i.e., unaccompanied voices.

Accelerando (It.). Accelerating (the tempo). Abbr.: *accel.*

Adagio (It.). Slow. *Adagietto*, faster than adagio; *Adagissimo*, slower than adagio.

Ad libitum (L.). At will; usually in reference to freedom of tempo. Abbr.: *ad lib.*

Affettuoso (It.). With affection, warm.

Affrettando (It.). Hurrying. Same as Accelerando. Abbr.: *affret.*

Agitato (It.), *Agité* (Fr.). Agitated.

Aimable (Fr.). Amiable.

Alcuna (It., fem.). Some. E.g., *Con alcuna licenza*, with some freedom.

All', Alla (It.). To, at, on, with the; in the manner of.

Alla Breve (It.). A tempo indication used with the signature ₵, implying a half-note unit at moderate to fast speeds.

Allant (Fr.). Going along (in tempo). See Andante. Also *Allant grandissant*, going on (in volume). Louder.

Allargando (It.). Broadening, slowing down, fuller in tone. Abbr.: *allarg.*

Allegro (It.). Cheerful, bright tempo. *Allegretto* indicates a tempo slightly slower than allegro.

Allmählich (Ger.). Gradually; used with other terms.

Allora (It.). Then.

Amabile (It.). Amiable.

Amoroso (It.). Amorous.

Ancora (It.). Once more, still more, even. E.g., *Ancora piu piano*, even more soft.

Andante (It.). A "walking" tempo, neither fast nor slow. Lies between allegretto and adagio. *Andantino* usually indicates a tempo slightly faster than andante.

Anfang (Ger.). Beginning (of the piece). *Vom Anfang*, back to the beginning again. Same as Da capo.

Anhang (Ger.). Ending. Same as Coda.

Animando (It.). Animating.

Animato (It.), *Animé* (Fr.). Animated.

Anschwellend (Ger.). Swelling (in volume).

Anwachsend (Ger.). Growing louder. Same as Crescendo.

Aperto (It.). Open, clear, broad in style.

A piacere (It.). As you like, free. See Ad libitum.

Appassionato (It.). Impassioned.

Appena (It.). Scarcely; used with other terms.

Assai (It.). Very; used with other terms.

Assez (Fr.). Enough, very; used with other terms.

A tempo (It.). In tempo (after some deviation).

Attacca (It.). Begin the next section immediately.

Au (Fr.). To the; used with other terms.

Auf (Ger.). On; used with other terms.

Aufhalten (Ger.). To hold up, to slow down.

Aus (Ger.). From; used with other terms.

Ausdruck (Ger.). Expression. *Ausdrucksvoll,* expressive.

Ausgehalten (Ger.). Held out, sustained.

Aussi (Fr.). As; used with other terms.

Basso Continuo (It.). In baroque music, the accompaniment played by the harpsichord or organ, together with one or more bass instruments.

Battuta (It.). Beat. E.g. *Ritmo di tre battute*, meter of three beats, expressed as measures, one beat to a measure.

Bedächtig (Ger.). Thoughtful, careful.

Bedeutend (Ger.). Significant, with meaning.

Belebter (Ger.). More animated.

Belustigend (Ger.). Gay.

Ben, bene. (It.). Well; used with other terms.

Beruhigend (Ger.). Quieting down.

Beschleunigen (Ger.). To accelerate the tempo. *Beschleunigt,* speeded up.

Bewegter (Ger.). More animated, more excited. Same as Piu animato.

Bien (Fr.). Well, very; used with other terms.

Breit (Ger.). Broad.

Brillant, brillante (Fr., masc. and fem.), *Brillante* (It.). Brilliant.

Brio (It.). Brilliance, spirit.

Brumeux (Fr.). Hazy, misty.

Buée (Fr.). Mist.

Cadenza (It.). A free section for a soloist, during which the accompaniment is silent. The style should be that of an improvisation, without strictness of rhythm. Abbr.: *cad.*

Calando (It.). Quieting down, usually in both dynamics and tempo.

Calcando (It.). "Trampling." Similar to Accelerando.

Calmato (It.). Calmed.

Calore (It.). Warmth.

Cantabile (It.). In a singing style.

Cantando (It.). Singing. Same as Cantabile.

Caressant (Fr.). Caressing.

Carezzando, carezzevole (It.). Caressing, caressingly.

Cedez (Fr.). Yield, give way a little. Slight ritardando.

Chaleur (Fr.). Warmth.

Chantant (Fr.). Singing. Same as Cantabile.

Chiaro (It., masc.). Clear, distinct.

Coda (It.). Ending (of the piece).

Col, coll', colla, colle (It.). With the; used with other terms. E.g., *colla parte*, with the part (an indication reminding the accompanist to stay together with the soloist).

Come (It.). As; used with other terms. E.g., *come prima*, as at first.

Comodo, commodo (It.). Comfortable tempo.

Con (It.). With; used with other terms.

Concitato (It.). Excited, aroused.

Continuo (It.). See Basso Continuo.

Crescendo (It.). Increasing (in volume). Abbr.: *cresc.* Sign: ⟨

Cupo (It.). Dark, somber.

Da (It.). Of, from; used with other terms. E.g., Da capo, from the beginning.

Debile (It.), *débile* (Fr.). Weak.

Decidé (Fr.), *Deciso* (It.). Decided, decisive.

Declamando, declamato (It.). In declamatory style.

Decrescendo (It.). Decreasing (in volume). Abbr.: *decresc.* Sign: ⟩

Delicato (It.). Delicate.

Deutlich (Ger.). Distinctly, well articulated.

Diminuendo (It.). Diminishing (in volume). Same as Decrescendo. Abbr.: *dim.* Sign: Same as for Decrescendo.

Di nuovo (It.). Anew.

Divozione (It.). Devotion.

Doch (Ger.). Yet, still.

Dolce (It.). Soft, sweet. *Dolcissimo*, very soft, very sweet.

Dolente (It.). Sad, doleful.

Dolore (It.). Grief. *Doloroso*, full of grief.

Doppio (It.). Double. E.g., *doppio movimento*, double speed.

Douce, doux (Fr., fem. and masc.). Soft, sweet.

Douleur (Fr.). Sadness.

Douloureux (Fr., masc.). Dolorous, sorrowful.

Drammatico (It.). Dramatic.
Drängend (Ger.). Pressing forward.
Dringend (Ger.). Pressing, urgent.
Drohend (Ger.). Menacing.
Duftig (Ger.). Misty.
Dureté (Fr.). Hardness.
Durezza (It.). Hardness (of tone or expression) .

Éclatant (Fr.). Brilliant, pompous, flashy, piercing.
Eilend (Ger.). Hurrying.
Eilig (Ger.). Speedy.
Einfach (Ger.). Simple.
Élan (Fr.). Dash.
Élargissant (Fr.). Broadening.
Elegiaco (It.). Elegiac.
Empfindung (Ger.). Feeling, sensitiveness.
Enchainez (Fr.). Connect with the section to follow. Same as Attacca.
Energico (It.). Energetic.
Entrain (Fr.). Vigor, dash.
Erlöschend (Ger.). Dying out.
Erweitert (Ger.). Broadened.
Espressione (It.). Expression.
Espressivo (It.). Expressive. Abbr.: *espress.*
Éteint (Fr.). Extinguished.
Etwas (Ger.). Somewhat, about (often used to qualify metronome
　　marks).
Expressif (Fr.). Expressive.

Facilement (Fr.), *Facilmente* (It.). Easily, fluently.
Fastoso (It.). Pompous.
Feierlich (Ger.). Solemn, festive.
Feroce (It.). Ferocious.
Fervore (It.). Fervor.
Feurig (Ger.). Fiery.
Flebile (It.). Weak, mournful.
Flehend (Ger.). Imploring.
Fliessend (Ger.). Flowing.
Flottant (Fr.). Floating.
Flüchtig (Ger.). Fleet, nimble.
Flüssig (Ger.). Fluid. Same as Fliessend.

Forte (It.). Loud, strong. *Fortissimo*, very loud. Abbr.: *f, ff*.

Forza (It.). Force. *Forzando*, forcing. *Forzato*, forced. Abbr.: *fz*. See Rinforzando and Sforzando.

Frais, fraîche (Fr., masc. and fem.). Fresh.

Freddo (It.). Cold, expressionless.

Frei (Ger.). Free.

Frenetico (It.). Frenzied.

Fresco (It.). Fresh.

Fröhlich (Ger.). Joyous, gay.

Fuoco (It.). Fire.

Furieux (Fr.), *furioso* (It.). Furious.

Gai (Fr.). Gay. *Gaiement*, gaily.

Gebunden (Ger.). Legato, smoothly connected.

Gedehnt (Ger.). Sustained.

Gefällig (Ger.). Pleasing, agreeable.

Gefühl, gefühlvoll (Ger.). Feeling, with feeling.

Gehalten (Ger.). Sustained, steady (in tempo).

Geheimnisvoll (Ger.). Mysterious.

Gehend (Ger.). Going along. See Andante.

Gemächlich (Ger.). Comfortable.

General pause (Ger.). A pause for the whole ensemble. Abbr.: **G.P.**

Gesangvoll (Ger.). In a singing style. Same as Cantabile.

Geschwind (Ger.). Swift.

Gesteigert (Ger.). Increased, heightened.

Getragen (Ger.). Sustained.

Gewichtig (Ger.). With weight, gravity, importance.

Giocoso (It.). Playful, humorous.

Giusto (It.). Correct. *Tempo Giusto*, correct tempo.

Glänzend (Ger.). Brilliant.

G. P., see General pause.

Gracieux (Fr., masc.). Graceful.

Grandezza (It.). Grandeur. *Grandioso*, with grandeur.

Grave (It., Fr.). Solemn, grave.

Grazia (It.). Grace. *Grazioso*, graceful.

Gusto (It.). Taste. *Con Gusto*, with tasteful expression.

Gut (Ger.). Good, well. E.g., *Gut gehalten*, well sustained.

Hastig (Ger.). Hurried, impetuous.

Heftig (Ger.). Violent.

Hervortretend (Ger.). Brought out, emphasized.
Hinsterbend (Ger.). Dying away.
Hurtig (Ger.). Swift, agile.

Immer (Ger.). Ever, still, always. E.g., *Immer schneller*, always quicker.
Incalzando (It.). Pressing forward.
Indeciso (It.). Undecided, halting, capricious.
Innig (Ger.). Heartfelt, intimate.
Istesso tempo (It.). The "same tempo" for the beat, although the meter may change (e.g., $\frac{2}{4}$ to $\frac{3}{4}$).

Joyeux, joyeuse (Fr., masc. and fem.). Joyous.

Klagend (Ger.). Lamenting, mourning.
Kläglich (Ger.). Mourning.
Klingend (Ger.). Resounding, resonant.
Kraft (Ger.). Strength.
Kurz (Ger.). Short (articulation).

Langoureux, langoureuse (Fr., masc. and fem.). Languorous.
Langsam (Ger.). Slow. Like Adagio.
Largamente (It.). Broadly.
Large (Fr.). Broad.
Largo (It.). Very slow, broad. *Larghetto*, not as slow or broad as Largo.
Lebendig (Ger.). Lively.
Lebhaft (Ger.). Vivacious.
Leger (Fr.). Light.
Leggiero (It.). Light. Abbr.: *legg.*
Leicht (Ger.). Light, easy. Same as Leggiero.
Leidenschaftlich (Ger.). Passionately.
Leise (Ger.). Soft, gentle.
Lent (Fr.), *Lento* (It.). Slow.
Liberamente (It.). Freely.
Licenza (It.). Liberty (in performance).
Lieblich (Ger.). With charm, pleasing.
L'istesso tempo (It.). See Istesso tempo. *Lo stesso*, modern Italian.
Lontano (It.). Distant.
Lourd (Fr.). Heavy.
Lusingando (It.). Flattering, intimate in style.
Lustig (Ger.). Cheerful.

Mächtig (Ger.). Powerful.

Maestoso (It.). Majestic.

Mancando, mancante (It.). Dying out.

Malinconico (It.). In melancholy style.

Marcato (It.). Marked, emphatic style.

Marziale (It.). March style. Martial.

Mässig (Ger.). Moderate.

Même (Fr.). Same; used with other terms.

Meno (It.). Less; used with other terms.

Mesto (It.). Mournful, sad.

Mezzo (It.). Half; used with other terms. E.g., *Mezzo forte*. The meaning "half" is not literally applied. Abbr.: *mf* (mezzo forte), *mp* (mezzo piano).

Misterioso (It.). Mysterious.

Moderato (It.). Moderate tempo, neither fast nor slow.

Modéré (Fr.). Moderate (tempo).

Möglich (Ger.). Possible. E.g., *So rasch wie möglich*, as fast as possible.

Molto (It.). Very, or much; used with other terms.

Morbido (It.). Smooth, soft. *Con morbidezza*, with smoothness, softly.

Morendo (It.). Dying away.

Mosso (It.). Moved (in tempo).

Moto (It.). Motion.

Müde (Ger.). Languid, tired.

Murmelnd (Ger.). Murmuring.

Mystérieux (Fr.). Mysterious.

Nach belieben (Ger.). Freely. See Ad libitum.

Nachgehend (Ger.). Following. See Colla parte.

Nachlassend (Ger.). "Leaving behind." Relaxing the tempo.

Nicht (Ger.). Not; used with other terms.

Nicht schleppend (Ger.). Not dragging.

Non (It., Fr.). Not; used with other terms.

Non tanto (It.). Not so much; used with other terms.

Non troppo (It.). Not too much; used with other terms.

Nobilmente (It.). With nobility.

Oppure, ossia (It.). Or. Used to indicate optional versions.

Parlando (It.). With the distinctness of speech.

Peine (Fr.). Used in the expression *A peine*, scarcely, hardly.

Perdendo, perdendosi (It.). Dying away gradually.

Pesant (Fr.), *Pesante* (It.). Heavy, rough.

Peu (Fr.). Little; used with other terms. *Peu a peu*, little by little.

Piacevole (It.). Likeable, agreeable.

Piangendo (It.). Weeping. *Piangevole*, plaintive.

Piano. (It.). Soft. *Pianissimo*, very soft. Abbr.: *p, pp.*

Pieno, piena (It., masc. and fem.). Full; used with other terms E.g., *A voce piena*, with full voice.

Più (It.). More; used with other terms.

Plaisant (Fr.). Merry.

Plötzlich (Ger.). Suddenly.

Plus (Fr.). More; used with other terms.

Poco (It.). Little; used with other terms. *Pochissimo*, very little. Abbr.: *poch. Poco a poco*, little by little.

Poi (It.). Then, after; used with other terms. E.g., *Poi la coda*, then the coda.

Pomposo (It.). Regal, dignified.

Posé (Fr.). Steady, poised.

Precipitando, precipitoso (It.), *Précipité* (Fr.). Precipitously.

Pressez (Fr.). Press forward. Same as Accelerando.

Presto (It.). Fast. *Prestissimo*, very fast.

Prima, primo (It., fem. and masc.). First. E.g., *Prima volta*, first time; *Tempo primo*, first tempo.

Quasi (It.). Almost, as if; used with other terms.

Quieto (It.). Quiet.

Rallentando (It.). Slowing (down the tempo). Abbr.: *rall.*

Rallentissant (Fr.). Slowing down.

Rasch, rascher (Ger.). Quick, quicker.

Rauschend (Ger.). Rustling.

Ravvivando (It.). Enlivening (the tempo).

Redend (Ger.). Speaking. Similar to Parlando.

Religioso (It.). Religious in style.

Renforcez (Fr.). Reinforce, get louder.

Retenant (Fr.). Holding back. *Retenu*, held back.

Rinforzando (It.). Reinforcing. Applied to individual tones. May sometimes involve an entire phrase. *Rinforzato*, reinforced. Abbr.: *rfz.*

Risoluto (It.). Deliberate, firm.

Ritardando (It.). Holding back, slowing down the tempo. Abbr.: *ritard., rit.*

Ritenuto (It.). Held back. Sometimes means an immediate rather than a gradual slowing down. Abbr.: *rit.*

Ritmo di tre battute (It.) See Battuta.

Rubato (It.). Play freely. Some beats are "robbed" of part of their value, while others gain value.

Ruhig (Ger.). Quiet, peaceful.

Sanft (Ger.). Soft, mild, gentle.

Scherzando (It.). Playfully.

Scherzoso (It.). Playful, jokingly.

Schleppend (Ger.). Dragging.

Schmachtend (Ger.). Languishing.

Schnell (Ger.). Quick.

Schwer (Ger.). Heavy.

Schwindend (Ger.). Vanishing, dying away.

Schwungvoll (Ger.). Full of enthusiasm, spirited.

Scintillante (It.). Sparkling.

Sciolto (It.). Free, easy style. (Sometimes, detached bowing.)

Scorrevole (It.). Flowing freely.

Sec (Fr.), *Secco* (It.). Dry (in tone and articulation).

Seconda, secondo (It., fem. and masc.). Second. E.g., *Seconda volta*, second time.

Segue (It.). "Follows." The next section follows immediately; or, continue playing in the same manner.

Sehnsuchtsvoll (Ger.). Ardent, full of longing.

Sehr (Ger.). Very, or much; used with other terms.

Semplice (It.). Simple.

Sempre (It.). Always, used with other terms.

Sentito (It.). With feeling.

Se perdant (Fr.). Disappearing. Same as Perdendosi.

Sereno (It.). Serene.

Serieux, serieuse (Fr., masc. and fem.). Serious.

Serré (Fr.). Pressed (ahead), growing faster. *Serrant,* pressing (ahead).

Seufzend (Ger.). Sighing.

Sforzando (It.). Forcing (an individual note). Abbr.: *sfz.*

Sforzato (It.). Forced. Abbr.: *sfz.*

Simile (It.). "Similarly." Continue in the same manner. Abbr.: *sim.*

Singend (Ger.). Singing. Same as Cantabile.

Slancio (It.). "Impetus." *Con slancio*, with impetuosity.

Slentando (It.). Slowing down.

Smorzando (It.). Dying away. Abbr.: *smorz.*

Soave (It.). Soft, gentle.

Sofort (Ger.). Immediately.

Solennel (Fr.). Solemn.

Sordamente (It.). Muffled, as though muted.

Sospirando (It.). Sighing.

Soutenu (Fr.). Sustained.

Sostenuto (It.). Sustained, usually with a broadening of tempo. Abbr.: *sost.*

Sotto (It.). Under. *Sotto voce*, subdued volume, whispering.

Soupirant (Fr.). Sighing.

Sourd (Fr.). Muffled, as though muted.

Sperdendosi (It.). Dying away gradually. Same as Perdendosi.

Spiritoso (It.). Spirited.

Stanco (It.). Tired.

Stark (Ger.). Strong. E.g., *Stark anblasen*, blow strongly (for wind instruments).

Stentando (It.). "Laboring." Slowing down, as though with effort.

Sterbend (Ger.). Dying away.

Stets (Ger.). Steadily, always; used with other terms.

Strepitoso (It.). Noisy.

Stretto (It.). "Drawn together"; i.e., suddenly faster.

Stringendo (It.). Speeding up. Same as Accelerando. Abbr.: **string.**

Stürmisch (Ger.). Stormy, impetuous.

Suave (Fr.). Suave, sweet.

Subito (It.). Suddenly, immediately; used with other terms.

Suivez (Fr.). Follow. See Colla parte.

Tant (Fr.). As much, much; used with other terms.

Tanto (It.). So much. See Non tanto.

Teneramente (It.). Tenderly.

Tranquillo (It.). Tranquil, quiet.

Trattenuto (It.). Held back. Abbr.: *tratt.*

Träumerisch (Ger.). Dreamy.

Traurig (Ger.). Sad.

Très (Fr.). Very; used with other terms.

Triste (It. and Fr.). Sad.

Troppo (It.). Too much. See Non troppo.

Unmerklich (Ger.). Imperceptible.

Un peu (Fr.). A little.

Unruhig (Ger.). Restless.

Vaporeux (Fr.). Vaporous, hazy.
Veloce (It.). With velocity, fast.
Verbreitern (Ger.). Broaden.
Vergnüt (Ger.). Joyous, cheerful.
Verlöschend (Ger.). Dying out.
Vif, vive (Fr., masc. and fem.). Lively.
Vigoroso (It.). Vigorous.
Vigueur, vigoureux (Fr.). Vigor, vigorous.
Vite (Fr.). Fast.
Vivace (It.). Vivacious, fast.
Vivo (It.). Lively.
Volante (It.). Flying, swift.

Wachsend (Ger.). Growing (louder).
Weich (Ger.). Soft, tender.
Wenig (Ger.). Little; used with other terms.
Werdend (Ger.). Becoming; used with other terms. E.g., *Langsamer werdend*, becoming slower.
Wie (Ger.). As; used with other terms. E.g., *Wie anfänglich*, as at the beginning.
Wohlgefällig (Ger.). Pleasant.
Wuchtig (Ger.). Weighty, forceful.
Würdig (Ger.). Dignified.
Wütend (Ger.). Enraged, furious.

Zart (Ger.). Tender, soft.
Zeitmass (Ger.). Tempo. *Im Zeitmass*, in tempo.
Ziemlich (Ger.). Rather; used with other terms.
Zögernd (Ger.). Hesitating, delaying. See Rallentando.
Zurückhalten (Ger.). Holding back.
Zuvor (Ger.). Before. E.g., *Wie zuvor*, as before.

MISCELLANEOUS SIGNS AND ABBREVIATIONS

Ornaments

Modern composers usually write out in exact note-values all kinds of small melodic flourishes which are ornamental in nature. But in earlier times (particularly the seventeenth and eighteenth centuries), certain signs were used for characteristic melodic formulas. The correct interpretation of many of these signs became obscure during

the nineteenth century, and their true meanings have only recently
been restored by modern scholarship. For the meanings of the ornament signs in Bach, Couperin, or other baroque composers, see the
authoritative articles by Putnam Aldrich under various headings in
the *Harvard Dictionary of Music*.

The following signs are practically the only ones found in nine-
teenth-century or contemporary music, and the methods of performance given here apply only to their uses in the music of these
periods:

1. *Grace Notes* (notes written smaller than the normal size).
Notes of very short duration, which, in modern usage, take some
of the value of the preceding note.

2. *The Trill*. Sign: tr. Rapid alternations of the written note
with its upper neighbor. In modern usage the trill begins with the
main note. Trills often end with grace notes involving the lower
neighbor.

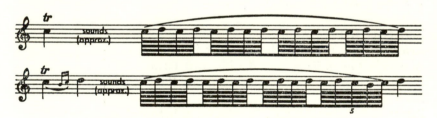

Trills may also be performed in continuous chains.

3. *The Turn*. Sign: ∿. This ornament involves a rotation between upper and lower neighbors of the main tone. When the sign
is directly over the note, the upper neighbor begins the ornament.

When the sign is between two notes, it fits in approximately as follows:

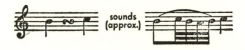

Abbreviations

Certain abbreviations are employed to reduce the effort in musical handwriting, and to save space. Some of them are:

1. *Tremolo.* Sign: many slashes across the note stem ♪. A real tremolo consists of very rapid unmeasured repetitions of a tone (see discussion of the string bowing in Appendix II, page 218).

2. *Measured Repetitions of a Single Tone.* Not to be confused with tremolo are abbreviations for tone repetitions in definite note-values. In writing these abbreviations the notes indicate the total durations of the abbreviated groups, and the slashes across the stems indicate the speeds of the repeated notes (one slash = eighth notes, two slashes = sixteenth notes, etc.).

3. *Tremolo Legato* (unmeasured). Rapid alternation between two tones, similar to a trill, but usually at an interval wider than a second. Each note is written with the value of the whole group, and many slashes are placed between the notes, not touching the stems.

Durations of the
tremolo groups.

With half-note values regular beams may be used instead of slashes. The abbreviation "trem." placed above the group prevents confusion with the measured two-tone repetitions discussed below.

or better

trem.

4. *Measured Repetitions of Two Tones.* Measured figures alternating two tones are shown by real beams connected to the stems, by slashes, or by combinations of beams and slashes indicating the speeds of the tones. Each note is written with the value of the whole group. Here are some examples:

sounds

sounds

The latter case may possibly be confused with unmeasured tremolo. This makes it still more desirable that the abbreviation "trem." be written above the group when a real tremolo is required. One may then assume, in the absence of this indication, that a measured group is intended.

Measured two-tone repetitions may be played legato (with slurs), or in detached style (without slurs).

5. *Repeated Figures.* When a figure involving more than two notes is repeated a number of times, slashes equaling the number of beams used in the figure may indicate its repetition.

6. *Repeated Bars.* The repetition of a whole measure is shown by the sign .

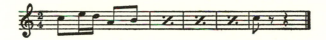

7. *Repeated Groups.* If the group to be repeated is of such proportions that one of the above signs will not cover it, and it still is not large enough to justify the use of a double bar with a repetition sign, a bracket over the group and the word "bis" may indicate the repetition.

8. *Rests of More than One Bar.* In parts for the individual players in orchestral or chamber music, long rests must sometimes be indicated. Modern practice favors the use of a wide, thick mark, with a number above the staff indicating the number of silent bars.

In some older editions there are specific rest signs (derived from whole- and breve-rests) which account for rests of two to eight bars. These signs are:

FOREIGN NAMES FOR TONES, ACCIDENTALS, MODES, AND NOTE-VALUES

Tones

The following chart gives Italian, French, and German names for the scale tones:

It.	do	re	mi	fa	sol	la	si
F.	Ut, or do	ré	mi	fa	sol	la	si
G.	C	D	E	F	G	A	H (B♭ is B)

Accidentals

	FLAT	SHARP	NATURAL	DOUBLE FLAT	DOUBLE SHARP
It.	bemolle	diesis	bequadro	doppio bemolle	doppio diesis
Fr.	bémol	dièse	bécarre	double bémol	double dièse
Ger.	Be	Kreuz	Quadrat, or Auf- lösungs- zeichen	Doppel-be	Doppel- kreuz

Italian and French terminologies add the name of the sign after the name of the note. German terminology for flatted and sharped tones is as follows:

FLATTED TONES	SHARPED TONES
Ces	Cis
Des	Dis
Es	Eis
Fes	Fis
Ges	Gis
As	Ais
B	His

Modes

	MAJOR	MINOR
It.	maggiore	minore
Fr.	majeur	mineur
Ger.	dur	moll

Terminology for Note-values as Used in England

Musical publications by English writers use an entirely different terminology for note-values from that used in the United States. Since students in this country do encounter English publications, it may be useful to list here the English names for the note-values. They are:

‖O‖   Breve

O   Semibreve

♩   Minim

♩   Crotchet

♪   Quaver

♬   Semiquaver

♬   Demisemiquaver

♬   Hemidemisemiquaver

Index

The foreign terms included in this index are only those used in the text. For others, see the glossary, pages 259–269.